Georgia O'Keeffe

These and other titles are included in The Importance
Of biography series:

Georgia O'Keeffe

by
Lois P. Nicholson

Lucent Books, P.O. Box 289011, San Diego, CA 92198-9011

Library of Congress Cataloging-in-Publication Data

Nicholson, Lois, 1949-
     Georgia O'Keeffe / by Lois P. Nicholson.
          p. cm.—(The importance of)
     Includes bibliographical references and index.
     ISBN 1-56006-055-7 (alk. paper)
     1. O'Keeffe, Georgia, 1887-1986—Juvenile literature.
2. Artists—United States—Biography—Juvenile literature.
[1. O'Keeffe, Georgia, 1887-1986.]   II. Title.   III. Series.
N6537.039N53   1995
759.13—dc20   94-37156
[B]   CIP
                                                             AC

Copyright 1995 by Lucent Books, Inc., P.O. Box 289011,
San Diego, California 92198-9011

Printed in the U.S.A.

Contents

Foreword

THE IMPORTANCE OF biography series deals with individuals who have made a unique contribution to history. The editors of the series have deliberately chosen to cast a wide net and include people from all fields of endeavor. Individuals from politics, music, art, literature, philosophy, science, sports, and religion are all represented. In addition, the editors did not restrict the series to individuals whose accomplishments have helped change the course of history. Of necessity, this criterion would have eliminated many whose contribution was great, though limited. Charles Darwin, for example, was responsible for radically altering the scientific view of the natural history of the world. His achievements continue to impact the study of science today. Others, such as Chief Joseph of the Nez Percé, played a pivotal role in the history of their own people. While Joseph's influence does not extend much beyond the Nez Percé, his nonviolent resistance to white expansion and his continuing role in protecting his tribe and his homeland remain an inspiration to all.

These biographies are more than factual chronicles. Each volume attempts to emphasize an individual's contributions both in his or her own time and for posterity. For example, the voyages of Christopher Columbus opened the way to European colonization of the New World. Unquestionably, his encounter with the New World brought monumental changes to both Europe and the Americas in his day. Today, however, the broader impact of Columbus's voyages is being critically scrutinized. *Christopher Columbus,* as well as every biography in The Importance Of series, includes and evaluates the most recent scholarship available on each subject.

Each author includes a wide variety of primary and secondary source quotations to document and substantiate his or her work. All quotes are footnoted to show readers exactly how and where biographers derive their information, as well as to provide stepping stones to further research. These quotations enliven the text by giving readers eyewitness views of the life and times of each individual covered in The Importance Of series.

Finally, each volume is enhanced by photographs, bibliographies, chronologies, and comprehensive indexes. For both the casual reader and the student engaged in research, The Importance Of biographies will be a fascinating adventure into the lives of people who have helped shape humanity's past and present, and who will continue to shape its future.

Important Dates in the Life of Georgia O'Keeffe

1887
Georgia O'Keeffe is born on November 15 in Sun Prairie, Wisconsin, where her father is a farmer.

1903
Moves to Williamsburg, Virginia, with her family.

1905-1906
Studies at the Art Institute of Chicago.

1907-1908
Attends the Art Students League in New York.

1908-1909
Works as a freelance illustrator in Chicago.

1912-1914
Teaches art in a public school in Amarillo, Texas.

1914-1915
Studies art under Arthur Dow at Columbia University Teachers College in New York.

1916
Alfred Stieglitz first exhibits O'Keeffe's work in New York.

1916-1918
Teaches art at West Texas State Normal School.

1917
Visits New Mexico for the first time.

1918
Moves to New York and begins painting full-time.

1923
Opens a successful one-woman show at New York's Anderson Galleries.

1924
Marries Alfred Stieglitz.

1928
Sells a series of calla lily panels for $25,000.

1933
Is hospitalized following a nervous breakdown.

1938
Travels and paints in Hawaii as a guest of the Dole Pineapple Company.

1943
The Art Institute of Chicago hosts O'Keeffe's first major retrospective.

1946
Alfred Stieglitz dies.

1946-1949
O'Keeffe oversees the distribution of Stieglitz's art collection.

1949
Elected to the National Institute of Arts and Letters.

1950
Moves to New Mexico permanently.

1951-1959
Travels extensively abroad.

1960
O'Keeffe's works displayed at the Worcester Art Museum in Massachusetts; largest O'Keeffe exhibit since 1946.

1965
Paints *Sky Above Clouds IV*, the largest painting of her career.

1970
New York's Whitney Museum opens a major retrospective of O'Keeffe's work.

1976
Publishes her autobiography, *Georgia O'Keeffe*.

1986
Dies on March 6 at age ninety-eight.

An Enduring Vision

"The meaning of a word—to me—is not as exact as the meaning of color. Colors and shapes make a more definite statement than words . . . where I was born and where and how I lived is unimportant," Georgia O'Keeffe wrote in her autobiography. "It is what I have done with where I have been that should be of interest."[1] In both the written and spoken word, O' Keeffe used language economically, yet she expressed herself eloquently and precisely. In her paintings too, O'Keeffe's voice speaks to the viewer with an unprecedented power of simplicity. Her works live as a visual testimony of an enduring spirit in American art. Her work and her example as a female artist are important: Her art defined the essence of America and her acceptance as a female artist proved that women could succeed in nontraditional roles.

Georgia O'Keeffe's presence in the history of American art is vital for several reasons. Her courage in being true to her inner vision lives as her most lasting gift to all who strive to listen to their intuitive natures in the face of established conventions. O'Keeffe accomplished this feat by staying the course of her singular vision. She would not be swayed by outside forces, and she gracefully accepted the cost of such dedication.

Georgia O'Keeffe's art was uniquely American in its subject matter. She advanced both the acceptability of American topics and the cause of women.

By heeding her own wise counsel, O'Keeffe became America's artist, capturing a wide array of the country's natural wonders. She cast aside tradition and expanded the smallest flower, painting it on such a grand scale that the eye was drawn

In 1970 an elderly O'Keeffe stands in front of her works Cross by the Sea *and* Deer's Skull with Pedernal *at the Whitney Museum of Art in New York City.*

to elements of nature that had previously gone unnoticed. Animal bones, left to bleach in the desert sun, not only served as tools for viewing the sky, but they came to personify the pioneering American spirit. Juxtaposed against the colors of the American flag, these artifacts symbolized the great diversity of America's landscape, celebrating the vastness of its character.

O'Keeffe's profound influence on art began just as women were granted the right to vote by passage of the Nineteenth Amendment in 1920. The critical acclaim that she gathered won her respect and ac-

ceptance in a male-dominated realm. Her bold art and style, and her willingness to break the established rules, encouraged other women to listen to their intuitive instincts as she had done. Critic Robert Hughes wrote, "No other American artist, and few living painters, have fused their inner and outer worlds with such spare grace. The life and work are one."[2]

Today, a new generation of art lovers has discovered Georgia O'Keeffe's works. Her paintings and the example of her courage endure as a testimony to this remarkable woman and artist.

1 Color, Light, and Pattern

Georgia Totto O'Keeffe was born in a farmhouse in Sun Prairie, Wisconsin, a small town near Madison, on November 15, 1887. The second child of Ida and Francis "Frank" O'Keeffe, she was named for her Hungarian grandfather, George Totto. A son, Francis Calyxtus O'Keeffe Jr., had been born two years earlier. The infant Georgia had her mother's dark hair and her father's round Irish face.

From an early age, Georgia was fascinated by light and color. She clutched at the particles of earth she saw swirling in the air in their dusty driveway, and she tried to taste them. Later, as an artist, she fantasized about tasting her oil paints as she squeezed them from the tube onto her glass palette.

From the beginning, Georgia was acutely aware of her surroundings. Indeed, her remarkable sense of visual memory extended as far back as infancy. It was the custom during that time not to expose young babies to the frigid Wisconsin winters, so Georgia remained in the house from the day she was born until May 1888, when she was carried outside for the first time. The memory of her first exposure to the bright sunlight at the age of just six months remained with Georgia throughout her life. Out on the lawn, she was placed on a handmade quilt and propped up by pillows. She remembered the quilt's patterns of red and white flowers on a black background and tiny red stars on a white background. She retained the image of her mother's friend Winnie, whose curly blond hair and long dress with blue flowers Georgia later described in vivid detail. She also was struck by the brightness of the sun and the glare it created as it

The farmhouse in Sun Prairie, Wisconsin, where Georgia O'Keeffe was born. From birth, O'Keeffe displayed a remarkable visual memory.

beat upon the white farmhouse. As Georgia squinted, she was aware of the shadows creeping from the tall hedge as if reaching for her.

No one would have believed that such a young infant could remember such things, but when Ida listened to her daughter's memories of the event years later, she admitted that they were extremely accurate.

At age six, Georgia sneaked into the parlor where Grandmother O'Keeffe kept her whatnot, a piece of furniture holding objects of interest. Fascinated by a clamshell, Georgia gently cradled it in her hands and held it against her ear to hear the ocean's roar. She loved its smooth lines and the feel of its cool surface.

Georgia grew up with a vivid impression of the Wisconsin landscape. She walked the cornfields with her father and used her shoulders to measure the corn's growth. She was fascinated with the changes each season brought to the land. She later described the fields bordering their farmhouse: "I remembered the beautiful fields of grain and wheat out there like snow—only yellow . . . in spring. . . . They were plowing and there were patterns of plowed ground and patches where things were growing."[3]

A Changing Society

Georgia was born into a rapidly industrializing society, although life in rural Sun Prairie was not affected by these changes. The Wisconsin farmers kept rhythm with nature while President Grover Cleveland fought to improve the lot of factory workers, immigrants and native-born alike, who labored under deplorable conditions. As Georgia's father sowed and harvested his crops, the Eiffel Tower was under construction in Paris and the Brooklyn Bridge, the country's longest suspension bridge, had just been opened in New York.

Sun Prairie, Wisconsin, remained untouched by the rapid industrial revolution occurring in major cities in 1900.

Wisconsin in the 1880s

Georgia O'Keeffe and the American writer Willa Cather shared a common heritage. Each had lived on the midwestern prairies and each, in her own way, recorded her memories and love of the land. This is Cather's description of the prairie from My Antonia.

"As I looked about me I felt that the grass was the country, as the water is the sea. The red of the grass made all the great prairie the colour of wine-stains, or of certain seaweeds when they are first washed up. And there was so much motion in it; the whole country seemed, somehow, to be running. . . . I felt motion in the landscape; in the fresh, easy-blowing morning wind, and in the earth itself, as if the shaggy grass were a sort of loose hide, and underneath it herds of wild buffalo were galloping, galloping. . . . I wanted to walk straight on through the red grass and over the edge of the world, which could not be very far away. The light air about me told me that the world ended here: only the ground and sun and sky were left, and if one went a little further there would only be sun and sky, and one would float off into them, like the tawny hawks which sailed over our heads making slow shadows on the grass. . . . I was left alone with this new feeling of lightness and content. . . . I was entirely happy. Perhaps we feel like that when we die and become a part of something entire, whether it is sun and air, or goodness and knowledge. At any rate, that is happiness, to be dissolved into something complete and great."

As the wife of a successful farmer during the late Victorian era, Ida Totto O'Keeffe had a role vastly different from that of the women who had settled the Wisconsin prairie just a generation earlier. Living in towns meant that women did not need the pioneer skills required of their mothers. Freed from many labor-intensive duties, women could devote more of their time to intellectual and cultural pursuits. They congregated and formed interest groups such as literary circles. As this new generation of American females emerged, Catherine Beecher made the following observation in an issue of the *American Home* in 1869:

> The race of strong, hardy, cheerful girls . . . that could wash, iron, brew, bake, harness a horse and drive him, no less than . . . embroider, draw, paint, and read innumerable books—this race of women, pride of olden time, is daily lessening.[4]

Women of the Victorian era were seen as delicate, demure creatures who were expected to be gentle and quiet, and dependent on their husbands for their financial security. They did not work outside the home, and many knew little about economic matters.

Ida O'Keeffe's Role

Ida O'Keeffe, however, had been raised differently. Her father had left the family, and her mother, Isabella Totto, had moved to Madison, a university town where more cultural opportunities existed for her daughters. A strong woman, Isabella managed the family's finances and taught her daughters to be independent. Based on her own experiences, Isabella instilled in her daughters the belief that women should be confident, self-sufficient individuals, capable of managing a household while seeking intellectual growth through reading, music, art, and other cultural interests. She was so successful in rearing daughters who shared her beliefs that only one daughter, Ida, ever married. Although she had hoped to become a physician, Ida took a special delight in raising five daughters who would retain the Totto women's strong, independent character.

The beautiful white farmhouse that Frank built for his bride, Ida, was soon full of children. Following Francis and Georgia came Ida Ten Eyck, born in 1888, Anita Natalie in 1891, Alexis Wycoff in 1892, Catherine Blanche in 1895, and Claudia Ruth in 1899. Ida's aunt Jane Wycoff, a widow, moved in to assist Ida, and Georgia remembered the firm "Aunt Jenny" as "the headache of my life. . . . I can see her now standing there with her hands clasped, inspecting her charges."[5]

A self-disciplined woman, Ida O'Keeffe was a stern, demanding parent who offered approval but did not cuddle her children. "As a child, I think I craved a certain affection that my mother did not give," said Georgia.[6]

To fulfill the role of eldest daughter, Georgia zealously assumed an air of authority. Her sister Catherine later recalled, "She was it. She had everything about her her way and if she didn't, she'd raise the devil."[7] Her younger sisters seemed to accept Georgia's dominant position. They shared bedrooms; Georgia had her own. "We paid no attention to it at all," Catherine said. "We all expected that she was always very nice to us all. She was a good older sister."[8]

From Georgia's perspective, things were quite different. She felt that her brothers were the favorite children in the family. However, Georgia acknowledged her strong sense of identity. "I had a sense of power," she said later. "I always had it."[9]

Life on a Wisconsin Farm

The O'Keeffe children had plenty of chores on the farm. Males and females were delegated different tasks because some work was not deemed appropriate for girls. Francis and Alexis milked the cows each day after school. The girls tended the vegetable garden, but they were not allowed in the barnyard. Defiantly, Georgia persuaded her sisters to sneak into the barn so that they could feel the cows' tongues. Georgia was different from the other children. Her creativity, daring, and desire to be alone made the family view her as an oddity.

Rural Wisconsin in the early 1900s proved an ideal place to grow up. Although all the O'Keeffe children had chores, they also had plenty of leisure time to pursue playing, exploring, and reading.

Laurie Lisle, one of Georgia O'Keeffe's biographers, described her subject's awkward role in the O'Keeffe family:

> She had lived with the annoying, but not painful, label of being the black sheep in the family, always being teased about her "crazy notions." As she matured, she discovered that no one minded at all when she gave her imagination free rein in colors and shapes.[10]

The O'Keeffe children enjoyed the usual leisure activities of children. They played hide-and-seek in the barns and spent hours on their swings. What Georgia liked best was playing alone with her dollhouse. She enjoyed her own company and the pleasure of being alone, later observing, "If only people were trees, I might like them better."[11]

Every evening the family congregated in the living room where Ida played the piano and read aloud to the children. "My mother was a great talker," Georgia said.

"She read to us on rainy days and weekends. . . . I think that reading was a good start to a lot of things."[12] Georgia loved sitting on the sofa and hearing stories about the West. She listened intently as her mother read aloud the tales of Natty Bumppo in James Fenimore Cooper's *The Pioneers* or *The Deerslayer*. As she listened, she imagined herself canoeing or scaling the eastern peaks with Deerslayer, Harry Hurry, and Chingachgook, the Indian chief. She also loved the adventures of Kit Carson in *The Life of Billy the Kid*.

The stories did more than nurture the children's love of reading, as O'Keeffe biographer Roxana Robinson observed:

> The tales did, of course, transmit historical information, but there was a philosophical message as well. Both the real-life adventurers and the fictitious heroes were advocates for the romantic cult of the individual. Romantic literature places power in the hands of the individual, not society. The message

A Farmer's Daughter

Everyone, including the children, had specific duties on the O'Keeffes' Wisconsin farm, and the daily routine seldom varied. In Georgia O'Keeffe: A Life, *Roxana Robinson describes life on the farm.*

"Days on the farm were full. Frank O'Keeffe came downstairs just after the hired girl had lighted the fires. He ate breakfast in the kitchen, with the hired men who would work beside him throughout the day. The women and children came down next, and while they ate in the dining room, the cook and the hired girl filled the children's lunch pails for school. . . . After school there were chores. The boys [tended the cows or horses]. . . . The large vegetable garden was tended by the children. . . .

Work was not the only outdoor activity. The children swung on the two big swings behind the house. . . . They were allowed to play [hide-and-seek] in the hayloft of the big barn. . . .

The girls made their own clothes and learned to cook on the cook's day off. . . .

Dinner was a quiet meal. . . . Afterward they all sat in the living room . . . where Ida would play the piano and sing. . . . There were games as well—dominoes or checkers—and often Ida read aloud to the children. 'My mother was a great talker. She told wonderful stories,' Georgia said. 'She read to us on rainy days and weekends. My older brother had bad eyes, and she'd read to him, and I always listened, even after I could read myself. I think that reading was a good start to a lot of things.'"

conveyed by these triumphant heroes was that the individual has the power to act, to alter lives, to triumph over adversity, and to emerge victorious. The message was not lost on the listening children.[13]

In 1898 Frank's brother Bernard died of tuberculosis, leaving his farm to Frank, who now had 640 acres to work. Frank's second brother, Boniface, had died ten

years earlier. This amount of land required a great deal of labor, and O'Keeffe needed the help of his sons. Thus a conflict developed between husband and wife. Ida deeply valued education, and she wanted the best instruction for her children. Frank, who wanted their two sons to become farmers, questioned the value of advanced training for the boys. Ida, however, insisted that all the children be well educated. Eventually, the boys went to military schools and the girls to convents for part of their education.

Frank O'Keeffe possessed an adventurous nature, and he brought some of that spirit to farming. He was one of the first farmers to have a telephone installed; it hung on the parlor wall. He persuaded his neighbors to buy subscriptions to the service, had the necessary poles erected to support the telephone cable, and even helped string the phone lines. Frank's progressive thinking extended into agriculture as well. He experimented with a crop of tobacco. If the desire to travel moved him, he acted on it. "I think that deep down I am like my father," Georgia reflected. "When he wanted to see the country, he just got up and went."[14]

Georgia Matures

Georgia quickly matured to become an independent, free-spirited young woman.

Later she attributed these qualities to the intense rivalry she felt with her brother Francis. "It may have come from not being the favorite child and not minding that— it left me very free," Georgia observed. "My older brother was the favorite child, and I can remember comparing myself to him and feeling I could do better."[15]

While she did not feel a sense of rivalry with her sisters, Georgia always strove to be different from them. If they wore white stockings and colored sashes, Georgia wore colored stockings. If her sisters braided their hair, Georgia wore hers loose. Rejecting bows and frills, she preferred an unadorned look, and she tried unsuccessfully to convince the others that they would also look better in this style.

Georgia was not physically attractive. Her strong, overly wide mouth seemed to fit her personality. Her features exuded strength of character. She considered herself an adult and disliked her prominent dimples, thinking they made her appear childish.

O'Keeffe, pictured with her brother Francis, attributed her independent spirit to her rivalry with her older brother.

When she entered the public school, Georgia found it boring. She kept to herself most of the time, occasionally erupting in class with challenging questions. Ida decided to enhance the children's education with experiences in the arts.

Early Artistic Training

Beginning at age nine, Georgia began formal training in art. At first, a teacher from the Town Hall School gave the O'Keeffe sisters lessons at their home in the evenings. Georgia discovered a picture that she liked a great deal in one of her mother's books, a small pen-and-ink drawing called *Maid of Athens*. Georgia was intrigued by its simplicity of line, and it motivated her to create similar drawings. Georgia also took piano and violin lessons, beginning a lifelong love of music.

Later Ida O'Keeffe arranged for more advanced art lessons. Each Saturday when Georgia was eleven, she was driven by buggy with her sisters Ida and Anita to the home of Sarah Mann, an art teacher in Sun Prairie. Mrs. Mann, a watercolorist, urged her students to duplicate paintings of art masterpieces in books. She taught her young students to apply colored paints to dampened paper. The Prang drawing book was popular at that time, and Georgia kept a copy of it on her nightstand. She and her sisters dutifully copied the shaded cubes and spheres in Prang's book. When Georgia was allowed to select the images that she wanted to draw, she chose deep red roses and spirited racehorses. Georgia learned how to use and care for an artist's tools: brushes, a palette, and paints. She developed a formal sense of light, color, and space on a flat plane.

Mrs. Mann corrected the students' work by painting directly on the pictures herself. This infuriated Georgia, who wanted nothing on her paper except her own efforts. Eventually these paintings were lost and Georgia claimed to be relieved.

One of Georgia's earliest memories of her watercolor classes was an attempt to draw a man. Georgia positioned him standing, lying on his back, and lying with his feet in the air. "I worked intensely—probably as hard as I ever worked at anything in my life," she remembered.[16] The images Georgia painted looked distorted to others. Instead of reproducing objects exactly as they appeared, Georgia gave them different colors. She emphasized a particular aspect of a scene such as a shape or line. Georgia was committed to producing what she visualized. She felt strongly about not conforming to the artistic standards of others.

Her Own Vision

A particular memory served to reinforce Georgia's early commitment to her own vision. She also remembered standing upstairs on a cold Wisconsin night and gazing out at a pointed spruce tree. Across the field she saw another tree silhouetted against the snow. There was an oak in the distance and then a line of woods. This bright moonlit scene with the dark, silent trees against the snow so impressed her that she began to draw it by lamplight. She wanted to capture the mood as well as the image.

Georgia was intrigued by the difference between actual color and the use of color

"I'm Going to Be an Artist"

When Georgia was twelve, playing with a friend, she asked the other girl what she wanted to be when she grew up. The friend responded that she did not know. "Well, I'm going to be an artist," Georgia announced. O'Keeffe biographer Laurie Lisle discusssed Georgia's decision in Portrait of an Artist: A Biography of Georgia O'Keeffe.

"In retrospect, Georgia never precisely put her finger on what prompted her at such an untried age to declare her intent to be an artist. No great women artists were mentioned in her school books, she didn't know any professional artists, and she cared little for the few paintings she had seen. But, as she observed in her book [*Georgia O'Keeffe*], a small illustration of a comely maiden in one of her mother's books had inspired her to create something as lovely herself. 'I think my feeling wasn't as articulate as that, but I believe that picture started something moving in me that kept on going and has had to do with the everlasting urge that makes me keep on painting,' she wrote. . . .

When she told the grownups that she was going to be an artist when she grew up, they humored what they regarded as a childish ambition by inquiring what kind of artist. Since Georgia didn't know that there were different kinds of artists, the only answer she could come up with . . . was 'a portrait painter.' When one of the adults remarked that sometimes she would have to paint ugly faces, Georgia became extremely irritated and emphatically denied it. To be an artist, in her evolving concept of the term, meant that she could do as she wished."

to achieve a mood. Explaining how she used colors differently, Georgia described painting the tree in the winter moonlight. "The bare trees were black against the snow in the moonlight, but dark blue had something to do with night."[17] She added dark blue to the black trees, and highlighted the strip of sky and color until it seemed "a sort of lavenderish grey."[18] For the snow, Georgia merely left the paper white. By altering the colors to express the mood of the composition, she had created a dramatic painting that evoked the feel of that moonlit winter night.

Leaving Home

In the fall of 1901, when Georgia was almost fourteen, she went away to the Sacred Heart convent, a boarding school outside of Madison. She later confessed it was the one year she ever learned anything. Freed from the constant criticism of her stern Aunt Jenny, Georgia blossomed at the convent, even earning a gold medal for her excellent deportment.

In addition to the annual $80 tuition, the O'Keeffes paid an extra $20 for Georgia to have art lessons, taught by Sister Angelique. The year's first assignment was to copy a white plaster cast of a baby's hand. Taking a stick of charcoal, Georgia firmly drew the lines of the hand. The more pressure she placed on the charcoal, the more ash fell over the drawing. Smudged and dirty, the picture still pleased Georgia as she handed it to Sister Angelique. The instructor, however, reprimanded her student for turning in such sloppy work. Then she showed Georgia how to make large sweeping lines. Humiliated, Georgia silently vowed to draw with larger, lighter strokes in the future.

By the end of the school year Georgia's paintings filled the school's art room. Sister Angelique had written "G. O'-Keeffe" in dark letters on all the drawings.

When she saw her name on the paintings, Georgia decided that she would never sign her pictures. Instead, she would create such distinctive work that the compositions would act as a signature. Years later, explaining why she never signed her works, she told an interviewer, "The meaning is there on the canvas. If you don't get it, that's too bad. I have nothing more to say than what I've painted."[19]

In 1902 Francis and Georgia were sent to a public high school in Milwaukee, where they lived with their aunt Lola, one of Ida's sisters. There was no local high school in Sun Prairie. This was Georgia's first exposure to city life, and it marked a significant change from life on the farm or in the convent. Teenagers in Milwaukee enjoyed a much freer existence than their rural counterparts. There was far less parental authority in the urban homes.

Georgia took an immediate dislike to her new art teacher for reasons that are not clear. One day, however, the instructor brought in a jack-in-the-pulpit and in-

Milwaukee, Wisconsin, at the time O'Keeffe lived and attended public high school there. O'Keeffe enjoyed the increased freedom from parental control that living in the city afforded her.

The Childhood Memories of an Artist

In her autobiography, Georgia O'Keeffe, *the artist remembered loving textures and colors as a young child.*

"My next memory must be of the following summer—the first memory of pleasure in something seen with my eye and touched with my hand. There was good-sized lawn all around our house. There was a long entrance drive with a high arborvitae hedge. I don't remember walking across the grass but I remember arriving at the road with great pleasure. The color of the dust was bright in the sunlight. It looked so soft I wanted to get down into it quickly. It was warm, full of smooth little ridges made by buggy wheels. I was sitting in it, enjoying it very much, probably eating it. It was the same feeling I have had later when I've wanted to eat a fine pile of paint just squeezed out of a tube."

structed the class about its marvelous structure, its form, and its deep, rich colors. Georgia had never considered drawing a plant and the idea fascinated her, but she resented the idea of someone she disliked so strongly introducing her to an activity she deeply enjoyed.

While Georgia and Francis attended school in Milwaukee, changes were occurring in the O'Keeffe family. Frank O' Keeffe, whose father and brothers had died of tuberculosis, lived in fear that he would also contract the dreaded disease. The extremely cold Wisconsin winters fu-

eled his fears, and he considered moving the family to a warmer climate. When a land developer convinced him that Williamsburg, Virginia, offered a healthier environment, Frank sold the farm in Sun Prairie for less than a dollar an acre. In 1903 Georgia set out with her family for a new life in Virginia.

Although she never lived in Wisconsin again, the land left a lasting impression on Georgia and always remained in her memory. For the rest of her life, she felt drawn to flat, open places and felt an affinity with the vast plane of sky and earth.

Chapter

2 A Budding Artist

When fifteen-year-old Georgia arrived with her family in Williamsburg, Virginia, in spring 1903, she found a beautiful town filled with magnificent trees of a kind she had never seen before. Her artist's eye took in the magnolia trees with their unusual glossy leaves, the lovely white flowering dogwoods, and the rich pink blossoms of the crape myrtles. The town was alive with pink and blue hyacinths, stars of Bethlehem, jonquils, and crocuses. The O'Keeffe family lived in a stately eighteen-room clapboard house, Wheatland, situated on nine acres, with an ample lawn and numerous porches for the children to play.

The O'Keeffes found southern culture vastly different from life in Wisconsin, where the virtues of hard work were sufficient to establish a place of respect in the community. The life of the American writer Willa Cather paralleled Georgia's life in many ways. As a child, Cather had also lived in Wisconsin and Virginia. Cather biographer Sharon O'Brien wrote, "Virginia was an old conservative society where life was ordered and settled, where the people in good families were born good and the poor mountain people were not expected to amount to much."[20]

In Williamsburg, the O'Keeffes found that everyone seemed to fit into a tightly

The O'Keeffe home in Williamsburg, Virginia. The O'Keeffes had a difficult time becoming accepted into Virginia society, which was very conservative.

organized social structure. From an early age, children were schooled in southern decorum (proper behavior). The O'Keeffe children were oblivious to these standards and felt no compulsion to follow them.

The townspeople viewed the O'Keeffes as a strange family. Frank and the O'Keeffe children did not concern themselves with the local customs, but Ida won acceptance by entertaining ladies for tea. She impressed them with her emerald earrings and her noble Hungarian heritage. But the people of Williamsburg thought Frank, who opened a grain store, distant and odd. According to strict southern custom, a gentleman did not engage in trade (run a store), nor did a gentleman actively farm, as Frank had done in Wisconsin. Thus the Virginians viewed their new neighbor, who lacked his wife's warm friendliness, as a lower-class worker. Frank soon became increasingly withdrawn and nervous, plagued by his obsessive fear of tuberculosis and mounting debts.

In the fall of 1903 Georgia's brother Francis entered the College of William and Mary, an all-male school in Williamsburg. Georgia enrolled at the Chatham Episcopal Institute, a girls' boarding school a few hundred miles away. Unlike many schools for young women, which focused on social skills, Chatham concentrated on academics. Georgia preferred plainness in her surroundings and in her own appearance. She liked the spartan interior of the school, where the students walked on unfinished floors, bathed weekly, and used an outdoor privy (toilet).

Georgia's Style

Georgia was not a beauty, but she possessed a quality that people noticed. Her dark skin, unadorned straight brown hair, and poker-straight posture drew attention. A classmate, Christine McRae, described Georgia's wide-set eyes as "pretty," and recalled, "Her features were plain—not ugly, for each one was good, but large and unusual looking. She would have made a strikingly handsome boy."[21]

Many Chatham students were away from home for the first time. Georgia had already spent two years away, however, and she was more self-assured than the others. "I started out not having any friends at all,"

she later wrote, "but I didn't pay any attention to it."[22] Despite her midwestern accent and peculiar ways, she became accepted and well liked. Known as "Georgie," she led pranks and taught her new friends to play poker. She was used to being the dominant eldest sister, and she enjoyed being in control and bossing the other girls. "When so few people think at all," she said to Christine McRae, "isn't it all right for me to think for them and get them to do what I want?"[23]

Freed from the strict atmosphere of the convent, Georgia's willful personality was unleashed. She later described this new freedom to Calvin Tomkins of the *New Yorker:*

> The atmosphere was entirely different from the convent. I used to stand there and think, "Now, what can I do that I

O'Keeffe's 1905 Chatham Episcopal Institute yearbook portrait. O'Keeffe's artistic skills blossomed at Chatham, where she was highly individualistic in her style.

shouldn't do and not get caught?" I'd go for long walks with another girl, which was not allowed. I had enough demerits to get expelled if I got one more. I wouldn't read my French lessons aloud three times to myself, as we were told to do; when they asked me whether I had done it I'd say no, I didn't have enough time for that.[24]

Chatham's principal, Elizabeth Mae Willis, served as the art instructor as well. A graduate of Syracuse University who had studied at the Art Students League in New York, she had directed the art department of the University of Arkansas. Willis immediately recognized Georgia's talent and displayed unusual tolerance for the tem-

peramental student's undisciplined work habits.

Christine McRae remembered Georgia as the queen of the art studio:

Her easel always stood in the center of the floor and was the high spot of interest. Here she would stand for hours, perfectly silent, working on something that seemed to us already finished, adding colors that our ordinary eyes could never see and serenely undisturbed by our incessant chatter as to how she got that purple, or the red, or the green. Presently, though, she would drop to earth, look around, and if Mrs. Willis was gone, spin on her heels, run up to somebody, give her a

---

"This Strong-Minded Girl"

The O'Keeffes moved to Williamsburg, Virginia, when Georgia was fifteen, and she attended Chatham Episcopal Institute. In her biography Roxana Robinson quotes a classmate of Georgia's, Christine McRae Cocke, who recalled Georgia's striking appearance.

"How vividly I recall the first night Georgia walked into study hall at Chatham Episcopal Institute! As I had been in school a few days, perhaps a week, I felt perfectly competent to criticize this late-comer, especially as she was unusual looking. The most unusual thing about her was the absolute plainness of her attire. She wore a tan coat suit, short, severe, and loose, into this room filled with girls with small waists and tight-fitting dresses bedecked in ruffles and bows. Pompadours and ribbons vied with each other in size and elaborateness, but Georgia's hair was drawn smoothly back from her broad, prominent forehead and she had no bow on her head at all, only one at the bottom of her pigtail. . . . Nearly every girl in that study hall planned just how she was going to dress Georgia up, but her plans came to naught, for this strong-minded girl knew what suited her, and would not be changed."

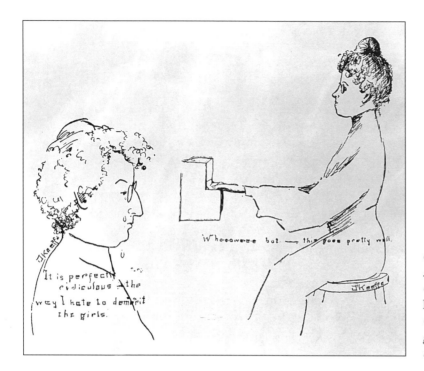

Georgia's sketches of the school's teachers for Chatham's yearbook, The Mortar Board. *By this time, O'Keeffe's artistic talents were gaining recognition throughout the school.*

hug and get the whole studio in an uproar. Then she would quiet down and by the time Mrs. Willis returned would be working away intently.[25]

Like many creative young people, Georgia found routines confining. She would work for a time, and then was apt to participate in childish pranks such as untying her classmates' hair ribbons. The other students complained that Mrs. Willis overlooked Georgia's antics. They were correct. Georgia later told a writer:

> Sometimes at school I would work hard and sometimes I wouldn't do a thing for days. Years later my teacher . . . told me that I had been her pet. I never felt I was anybody's pet. I think I interested her, and was sort of a problem to her.[26]

Unlike more traditional teachers, Willis encouraged Georgia to work at her own pace, arranging for her to return to

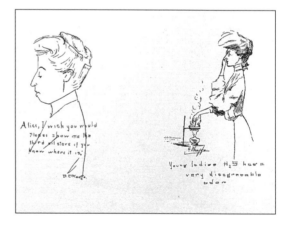

the studio in the evenings while the others studied. In her second year at Chatham, Georgia's talents were widely recognized. She was chosen art director of the yearbook, *The Mortar Board*, and filled the book with her own amusing caricatures of her teachers and classmates.

As graduation approached in June 1906, Georgia faced a challenge: She had

Three Women Who Influenced Georgia's Life

When Georgia decided to move to Chicago to pursue her education in 1905, she had begun to establish herself as an independent person, ignoring the conventions that governed most women's lives in that era. The influence of three powerful women is described by O'Keeffe biographer Roxana Robinson in Georgia O'Keeffe: A Life.

"The primary role model, of course, was Ida: as Virginia Woolf says, 'We think back through our mothers if we are women.' Georgia's mother was a figure of great authority and determination, who supported absolutely her children's aspirations and encouraged their self-reliance and effectiveness. Ida's high standards and expectations made Georgia's choice a logical one: serious study at a great institution, rather than a postgraduate year painting china and waiting to marry.

Next came Elizabeth Mae Willis, head of Chatham. . . . A woman of considerable depth and presence, she was broad-minded, perceptive, and effective. She had overcome the physical handicap of partial facial paralysis, and the psychological one of being female, to combine a rewarding professional career with a productive domestic life. Married and a mother, she raised her own children at home, taught all the art courses as well as running the school, and accomplished it all with dignity and wisdom.

Third in this trio of strong women was Aunt Ollie, with whom Georgia was to live in Chicago. . . . Ollie was possessed of a fierce independence, an abundant authority, and a trace of hauteur. 'There was something about Aunt Ollie,' said her grandniece Catherine Klenert Krueger. The 'something' was a touch of imperiousness, the expectation of excellence, and a brisk impatience with anything second-rate: intelligence, integrity, or effort."

to pass a spelling exam. After six attempts, she achieved a passing mark, but throughout her life her letters were peppered with misspelled words.

While the other Chatham seniors focused their attention on returning home in search of romance and marriage, Georgia had different goals. "I am going to live a life different from the rest of you girls," she proclaimed. "I am going to give up everything for my art."[27]

Although she had loved Williamsburg at first, Georgia now found its humidity and lush greenery suffocating. She longed for the prairie's open, flat spaces, where she could feel the wind and gaze out on vast horizons. But she realized that to become an artist, she needed more training, and that meant attending an art school in a major city.

The Art Institute of Chicago

Elizabeth Mae Willis encouraged Georgia to go to the Art Students League in New York, but Georgia's parents, familiar with the Midwest, wanted her to attend the Art Institute of Chicago. Ida O'Keeffe's sister Ollie and brother Charles lived together and were within walking distance of the Institute. Georgia could live with them while she attended school. Despite Georgia's independence, when she set out for Chicago in September 1905, not quite eighteen years old, she found the thought of moving to such a huge city intimidat-

ing. Recalling her fears, she later wrote, "When I was a youngster and was going away from home on the train—it was a very special sort of sick feeling."[28]

Georgia had always admired her mother's older sister Allietta, or Aunt Ollie. Staying with Aunt Ollie in Chicago strongly influenced Georgia. For the first time, she lived with a professional woman who had successfully made her way in a man's world. The oldest child of George and Isabella Wycoff Totto, Ollie had played a vital role in the Totto family. Roxana Robinson, one of Georgia O'Keeffe's biographers, describes Ollie Totto's accomplishments:

> During the 1890s, after her mother and sister Josephine died, Ollie moved to Milwaukee. There Ollie, amazingly and against all odds, became the only female proofreader at the *Milwaukee Sentinel.* This feat was much more celebrated within the family: the image of

Georgia began taking classes at the Art Institute of Chicago in 1905. At first intimidated by the level of sophistication of the other students, Georgia quickly rose to first in her class.

tiny, indomitable Aunt Ollie, with her aristocratic profile and regal posture, taking her triumphant place among the serried [crowded] ranks of disgruntled men was one in which they all exulted. Her attitude of fierce vigilance and her contempt for error made her brilliantly effective at her job. Aunt Ollie was famously self-sufficient; she maintained her own emotional and financial independence throughout her long and active life.[29]

On the first day of classes in Chicago, Georgia climbed the steep steps between the imposing bronze lions and entered the massive building. As she mingled with the other students in the Great Hall, she noticed that they all seemed older and more sophisticated. She felt like a young schoolgirl with her single plait fastened by a bow. Founded in 1879, the Art Institute followed the European tradition in which the students' works were ranked monthly by a numerical system. Those earning the highest scores set their easels up in the front of the class near the professor, while those receiving lower marks worked in the rear of the room.

The first lesson involved drawing the torso of an armless man from a plaster model. As Georgia worked, a young male student kept examining her work. Remembering Sister Angelique's teachings at Sacred Heart, Georgia used faint, sweeping strokes. When she glanced at the young man's drawing, she saw him using the bold, tight lines she had once attempted. The young man assured her that his method was correct. But, at the end of the day, Georgia smiled wryly when she was assigned to an advanced class, while her male critic remained in the lower section.

For the first time Georgia found herself among students who demonstrated impressive talents. Suddenly she felt inferior. Her confidence weakened even more the first time she saw a nearly nude male model, wearing only a loincloth, in an anatomy class held in a dark basement studio. Georgia wanted to run from the room as her faced turned deep red. But she realized that she would see many nude models in the required anatomy classes. Although men and women were taught separately, she found it difficult to overcome her self-consciousness and embarrassment. But she had to do it to remain in the school. Her courage was rewarded when, at the end of February, she was ranked first in her class.

Other aspects of Georgia's training proved more enjoyable. In a light, airy upstairs studio, she took a life drawing class taught by Professor John Vanderpoel, an accomplished artist. Vanderpoel taught by drawing large figures on tan paper with black and white crayons, reaching as high as he could with his short arms to complete a line. At the end of the year, Georgia ranked first in the class of twenty-nine women. Although Georgia learned a great deal from these classes, for the rest of her career she very rarely painted human figures.

Typhoid Fever

At the end of the school year Georgia boarded a train for Williamsburg to spend the summer with her family. But a few weeks after her return to Wheatland, she began to experience headaches and fever. Her illness was diagnosed as typhoid fever,

Chicago at the Beginning of the Twentieth Century

When Georgia arrived in Chicago in 1905, the city was experiencing a cultural renaissance, ignited by the Columbian Exposition of 1893. Emmett Dedmon provides a description of the artistic climate alive in the Chicago of a century ago in Fabulous Chicago: A Great City's History and People.

"After the turn of the century a new kind of commerce animated Chicago. From the prairie states that produced the grain and livestock which funneled through Chicago for the East came a sudden outpouring of writers, all of them attracted by the vigor and promise of the young city by the lake. . . . The period of their activity was brief. Like the hundreds of trains which daily snaked into Chicago's rail terminals, many paused only long enough to refuel—or perhaps to switch tracks or change to another line. But no one was to forget they had passed by. . . .

There would always be a transient quality about Chicago's relations with the arts. . . . 'It was a city,' said H. L. Mencken, which offered 'free play for prairie energy . . . some imaginative equivalent for the stupendous activity they were bred to.' "

Chicago was an artistic mecca when O'Keeffe was there in the early twentieth century. Its reputation drew many artists and writers.

a disease caused by a bacterium that often is prevalent in places having poor sanitation and contaminated drinking water. After several days of high fever, Georgia recovered. But the illness left her weak, frail, and depressed; the fever had caused her to lose her long, dark hair, and she wore a lace cap to conceal her baldness. When September arrived, she was still too weak to return to Chicago. She lay in a hammock, her skin sallow, her face thin and sad, as her brother and sisters departed for school. Amid the autumn splendor, she set up an easel in the yard and began to paint. In the winter she worked in a studio in the basement.

Occasionally her teacher at Chatham, Elizabeth Mae Willis, visited Georgia and continued to urge her to go to New York. But financial problems were mounting in the O'Keeffe home. The grain store was not prospering, and Ida had been forced to take in "table boarders"—male college students who ate with the family. By the summer of 1907, Frank O'Keeffe had closed the store and begun a concrete block construction business.

In view of the family's bleak financial outlook, Georgia decided to discontinue her studies and look for a job. She asked the Art Institute for a letter of recommendation to help her find work as an art teacher. The letter said, "Miss O'Keeffe is a young lady of attractive personality, and I feel that she will be very successful as a teacher of drawing."[30]

Ida O'Keeffe wanted Georgia to continue her studies, however, and she assured her daughter that the family could afford tuition. Indeed, by scrimping and saving money from the boarders, Ida scraped together just enough money for Georgia's studies. Georgia decided to go to New York, which was much more progressive than Chicago. When Georgia boarded the train in September for the twelve-hour trip to New York, she was glad to be leaving her problems behind. She had narrowly escaped death, and she eagerly anticipated the adventure of life in New York.

Chapter

3 The Nonconformist

Georgia felt liberated as she stepped from the train in New York City in September 1907. She immediately liked the city and felt she belonged. She was no longer the tentative seventeen-year-old who had felt alienated in Chicago.

As she searched for an inexpensive boardinghouse near her new school on West 57th Street, Georgia's style of hair and dress appeared almost futuristic. The look created by her dark hair, still growing out following the fever-induced baldness, would become fashionable in the 1920s. Georgia's customary loose-fitting clothing and uncorseted torso further served to give her the image of a modern, sophisticated woman.

Many of the students at the League lived in the boardinghouses then lining West 57th Street, where Georgia found a room costing only a few dollars weekly. She immediately fell into an easy camaraderie with the other art students. Soon, Georgia was known as "Patsy," a nickname often bestowed on individuals of Irish ancestry. The student body at the school was much smaller than at the Art Institute of Chicago, and Georgia found that even the building was less imposing. She immediately loved the natural light and openness of the upper-floor studios, where skylights invited the sun.

William Merritt Chase, a leading twentieth-century American artist, taught at the Art Students League, and it was Georgia's great fortune to have him for an instructor. His influence on Georgia would be profound and lasting.

While studying in Europe in the 1870s, Chase had adopted the bold, imaginative quality of the seventeenth-century Dutch and Spanish masters. Returning to the

O'Keeffe eagerly looked forward to studying at the Art Students League in New York City in 1907. The city was a busy metropolis even in the early twentieth century.

William Merritt Chase (below) was one of O'Keeffe's teachers at the Art Students League (left). Chase wanted students to complete a painting a day for a week.

United States, he quickly established himself as the favorite portrait artist of wealthy American families. Chase became a wealthy man, offering a sharp contrast to the more common image of the starving artist. Chase's studio on West 10th Street, filled with Chinese porcelain, valuable paintings, suits of armor, and tiger-skin rugs, was a popular hangout for New York's artists, who were greeted at the door by a black servant dressed in the attire of a Nubian slave.

At school Chase would sweep into the studio, dressed in a silk top hat, suede spats (shoe coverings), and gloves. He wore a flower in his lapel, and a monocle (single eyeglass). He challenged his young students to complete a painting a day for a week. Georgia observed that Chase made everything seem effortless. With a flick of his wrist, he could add just the right touch to a painting. "Making a painting every day must do something for you," she concluded.[31] Georgia found Chase "fresh, energetic and fierce and exacting, and fun."[32] Waltzing among the budding young painters, he would simultaneously encourage, criticize, and praise their efforts.

Georgia felt rejuvenated, but she was still plagued by financial concerns. When the other students returned to their homes for the Christmas holidays, Georgia remained in New York to save the train fare. She thought about modeling for other artists to earn money, but modeling was time-consuming and she wanted to devote time to her art.

In January 1908 an incident occurred that would live forever in Georgia's memory. As she climbed the stairs at the Art Students League one day, she met a handsome young student, Eugene Speicher, who teasingly halted her, begging Georgia to model for him. He told Georgia that she could not pass him on the stairs until she agreed. Georgia continued to refuse.

"It doesn't matter what you do," taunted Speicher. "I'm going to be a great painter and you'll probably end up teaching in some girls' school."[33]

Speicher's words stung. It was true that few female artists were seriously regarded during that era. But Georgia had vowed that she would not be like legions of other young women who sacrificed their personal ambitions for a husband and a family. She was willing to make that sacrifice for her art.

However, soon after the incident on the steps, Georgia, badly in need of money, relented and modeled for Speicher. She earned a dollar for four hours of posing at the League. Speicher entered his portrait

William Merritt Chase

At New York's Art Students League, William Merritt Chase taught Georgia O'Keeffe in 1907, leaving a lasting impression on his young student. For sheer joy in exciting brushwork and texture of paint, no American artist surpasses Chase. This appreciation is taken from Ronald G. Pisano's book William Merritt Chase.

"With the growing awareness and reassessment of the importance of nineteenth- and early twentieth-century art, William Merritt Chase (1849–1916) has emerged as a quintessential American artist. Not only did he champion the cause of the American artists, he also sought to establish an American Art statement. The work he produced is now recognized as a synthesis and summation of the many divergent art movements current at the turn of the century. Chase considered himself a 'realist.' The broad scope of his work, however, precludes simple classification. Included in [Chase's paintings] are works of great power and dynamism, as well as quiet, sensitive paintings with delicate nuances of character. He was acutely aware of artistic developments both in this country and abroad, and in his mercurial way he adopted stylistic elements from almost every artist worthy of attention. As a teacher of art, Chase instructed his pupils to do likewise, counseling them: 'Be in an absorbent frame of mind. Take the best from everything.' Through careful selection and clever amalgamation, he managed to create a composite style of his own, which has been described as eclectic but which is clearly recognizable as the 'style of William Merritt Chase.'"

In need of money, O'Keeffe agreed to model for Eugene Speicher, a handsome but arrogant young artist, who painted this portrait of the young woman in 1908.

of her, entitled "Patsy," in a League competition, where it won the school's Kelly Prize. One of the judges was Alfred Stieglitz, a famous photographer and an established figure in New York art circles, who called the painting "a swell head."[34]

Meeting Alfred Stieglitz

Impressed with Speicher's work, Georgia agreed to pose for him again in January. Halfway into the session, a group of male students dropped by the studio, inviting Speicher and his model to join them for a jaunt to Alfred Stieglitz's gallery at 291 Fifth Avenue, where some drawings by the great French sculptor Auguste Rodin were exhibited.

Georgia was the only female member of the group visiting the gallery. While she realized that she had been invited simply because she happened to be modeling at the time Speicher's friends dropped by, she possessed a curiosity about the Rodin drawings. Many years later, she vividly recalled the trip to the gallery. "On our way down to the gallery the men had said that they heard that he [Stieglitz] was a great talker, as they put it—they wanted to 'get him going.'"[35]

The young male artists had heard about Stieglitz's fiery temper and his impassioned speeches regarding art. They thought it would be great fun to engage him in such a discussion. Georgia later described the first time she saw Alfred Stieglitz:

Photographer Alfred Stieglitz was an impassioned patron of the arts. At his studio he frequently exhibited the works of other artists.

Alfred Stieglitz's studio on Fifth Avenue was a popular hangout for the students from the League. O'Keeffe first met Stieglitz at his studio.

My first memory of Stieglitz was on a day in 1908 when I was at the Art Students League. New York was covered with fresh snow. I went with two or three students to see the Rodin drawings at "291." "291" was a few rooms at that address on Fifth Avenue where a new kind of art was shown—and it was the only place in New York you could see anything like it. We went up the steps to the front door where we took a very small elevator and came out into a bare room—windows to the back. Stieglitz came out of a sort of dark place with something dripping water on the floor. He was a man with a shock of very dark hair standing straight up on top of his head—making his face look lean.[36]

As anticipated, the group of young men quickly drew Stieglitz into a spirited debate.

"Within minutes, the talk was heated and violent," remembered Georgia.[37] But such discussions bored Georgia. She found talk of ideas and philosophy a waste of time. She preferred to paint instead.

To get away from the men, she sauntered to the farthest end of the room. "I was tired and I didn't want to listen to them," she recalled. "There was no chair to sit on and nothing to do but stand and wait until we finally left."[38] As the group departed, the students acknowledged to one another that the older man had whipped them soundly in the debate.

Speaking Her Own Artistic Voice

Georgia returned from 291 that night with a feeling of growing alienation. She often felt different from others. Sometimes, it was because she was the only woman. At other times it was because she did not enjoy discussing what others discussed. But that same menacing feeling began to define the way she felt about her art. Not only did she dislike much of the work being done around her at the League, she also found herself trying to emulate the work of others such as William Merritt Chase. Although she could easily reproduce such styles, they did not seem natural to her. Such artistic convention was focused on a representational treatment of a subject, meaning that an exact likeness was painted, leaving little room for individual expression using light and shadow. But Georgia longed to paint subjects the way she perceived them. Later she remembered thinking, "I would like to make a picture I would really like."[39]

Alfred Stieglitz

Georgia O'Keeffe's work and Alfred Stieglitz's story became so interwoven that it is difficult to tell of one without including the other. When Georgia met Stieglitz in New York in 1908, she had no way of knowing the important role he would play in her life. Georgia's friend Anita Pollitzer provides some interesting background on Stieglitz in A Woman on Paper: Georgia O'Keeffe.

"This man, such a powerful force in photography and art in America for over half a century, was born in 1864, in what was then fashionable Hoboken, New Jersey, just across the river from New York. His was a cultivated, cultured family. When he was nine, they moved to New York City and Alfred, the eldest son, attended the Charlier Institute, an outstanding French-speaking private school, where great stress was laid on perfection of work and on fine penmanship. . . .

In winter the family lived in a brownstone house his father, Edward Stieglitz, had built on East Sixtieth Street. From spring to late fall each year, the family spent time in their summer home at Lake George in northern New York State. There, Alfred Stieglitz fell under the spell of the lake, the trees, the light and shades of nature.

At thirteen, he entered public school, and later, for two years, the College of the City of New York. In 1881, when he was seventeen, his father took the whole family to Europe to give his children the advantages of education on the Continent. . . . For three years [Stieglitz] studied at the University of Berlin. Photography became his passion.

He traveled with his camera throughout Europe, photographing constantly and entering prints in international competitions and winning many prizes. . . . At the age of twenty-six, already a recognized photographer, he returned to New York. . . . In 1905 Stieglitz opened a gallery at 291 Fifth Avenue, which became known in the United States and abroad simply as 291. . . . From the beginning, Stieglitz sought to dignify the profession of photography as an art form."

O'Keeffe and Stieglitz in later years, long after they had committed themselves to each other.

Although O'Keeffe painted Dead Rabbit and a Copper Pot *solely to please William Chase, it won her a scholarship to the League's summer school at Lake George, New York.*

In the 1870s a group of French painters had begun experimenting with different ways of depicting reality. The Impressionists painted tangible objects using a technique requiring hundreds of subtle dabs of color on the canvas. This treatment emphasized the way that light is reflected from surfaces, and while a subject remained recognizable to the viewer, an impressionist painting had a distinct quality.

As the twentieth century dawned, some painters moved even further away from representational art. These painters painted abstract figures, shapes, and forms in the way they perceived them, with no concern for representational convention. Georgia was attracted to these newer movements in artistic expression.

One evening Georgia walked with some students along Riverside Drive, on the west side of Manhattan. She was struck by the image of two trees against the night sky. Georgia painted the scene the next morning and was pleased with the results.

The painting, featuring two poplar trees reaching into the night with a wide expanse of dark sky separating them, was reminiscent of the strong style of Dutch painter Vincent van Gogh. Georgia enthusiastically showed her painting to a male student, who immediately began to advise her about how to improve it. Suggesting that the poplar trees needed a different treatment, he took his brush and repainted them. Although he had ruined the original work, he had also done Georgia a tremendous favor. She now realized that if she was to be a painter, she must paint to please herself.

At the end of the term, Georgia received a scholarship to the League's summer school at Lake George, New York. The scholarship was awarded as a prize for a still life painting done for William Merritt Chase's class. Ironically, the painting was not one Georgia particularly liked. To please her instructor, she had dutifully painted a dead rabbit lying beside a copper pot.

Discovering the Emotional Aspect of Art

Lake George, a popular resort in upstate New York, was an artists colony where painters, sculptors, and writers congregated. Georgia had a lovely room overlooking the lake, but she did not feel inspired to paint. "We had a sailboat with a red sail, the daisies were blooming, the mountains were blue beyond the lake," she recalled. "But it just didn't seem to be anything I wanted to paint."[40]

One evening a young man asked Georgia to sail with him on the lake. Georgia

Creating Her Own Visions

As Georgia sat in William Merritt Chase's class at the League, she discovered that art could be fun. However, she also knew that the still life paintings Chase emphasized were not satisfying to her as an artist. O'Keeffe biographer Jeffrey Hogrefe describes Georgia's feelings in O'Keeffe: The Life of an American Legend.

"It was a cathartic year for O'Keeffe. By copying the still-life arrangements of copper pots and slimy fish that Chase put out for his students, she came to believe, as Cézanne had already suggested, that colors could create a picture by interacting not only to define a subject but to evoke a universe of sensation.

For her, listening to Chase was like following a religious leader. . . . As O'Keeffe began to produce faithful renditions of Chase's work, however, she once again began to question what she was creating. Being an intuitive person, a daughter of a farmer, guided by an inner rhythm based on the rotation of the planet, she felt false merely imitating Chase's style. She felt her work was not from the heart. She wanted it to express the 'wideness and wonder of the world we live in.' When Chase told his students to try to paint the sky as if we could see through it, Georgia took his words to heart and experimented by applying white instead of the usual dark hues to the foundation of her canvas. The result was luminous—and it excited her. She wanted more light, more originality. She later reflected on her struggle: 'I saw that any idiot could come to copy another painting. I wanted to create a painting.' "

invited another male friend; both men, who had been vying for her attentions, seemed to pout all evening. As they sailed across the lake in heavy silence, Georgia concentrated on the dense brown marsh grasses near the shoreline. "In the darkness it all looked gloomy, very gloomy," she remembered.[41] This experience reinforced Georgia's childhood perceptions about emotions and visual representations. The two entities had to be aligned in the artist's soul. Suddenly, it struck Georgia that the entire visual world depended on the emotional world; feelings transformed visual reality into spiritual perceptions.

The next morning she returned to the shore to paint the marshes, attempting to recapture the mood of the preceding evening. She seldom gave away any of her paintings, but when one of the young men asked her for the picture, Georgia gladly gave it to him, grateful for the powerful revelation that had come to her on the lake.

When the summer ended, Georgia returned to Williamsburg. Frank O'Keeffe's business had failed, and the family now lived in a ramshackle house made of concrete blocks left over from that enterprise. They had been living on the income from the sale of the farm in Wisconsin, but those funds were nearly depleted. The new financial crisis meant that Georgia could not return to art school, nor her sisters to Chatham. Only Alexis was able to return to college.

Despite their economic woes, Ida O'Keeffe maintained an air of normalcy in her home. Georgia enjoyed being reunited with her family and took pleasure in their daily routines. But a letter written to Florence Cooney, her New York roommate, revealed her mounting concerns about money and her thoughts about earning a living.

Papa told me two or three days ago that he would send me back to the League if he could, but that he couldn't just now. I certainly like to please him. He is having hard luck these days but never says much because he doesn't like to own up to it, even if to himself. My private opinion is that the wisest thing for Pats [Georgia herself] to do is wake up . . . and see what she can do . . . I am going to get busy and see if I can do anything if I work regularly.[42]

As much as she loved her family, Georgia had become accustomed to living on her own and she soon found living at home to be suffocating. She recalled: "All the time I was at home it was always 'more of Georgia's crazy notions.' They didn't like the way I did my hair. . . . It finally got so at home I did what my mother wanted and when I was away I did as I pleased."[43]

On Her Own

Unable to go to school and unwilling to live with her family, Georgia returned to Chicago to look for a job. It was not her favorite city, but she could save money by living with Aunt Ollie and Uncle Charlie. She found work as a commercial artist with an advertising agency, drawing illustrations for ads and designing logos. She created intricate designs of lace for department store ads and designed a famous symbol for a popular kitchen cleanser: the Little Dutch Girl. But the work allowed for no imagination or use of her creative talents,

The concrete block house in Williamsburg that the O'Keeffes were reduced to living in after Frank's business failed.

and Georgia hated it: "I could make a living at it. . . . That is I could exist on it—but it wasn't worth the price—Always thinking for a foolish idea for a foolish place didn't appeal to me for a steady diet."[44] Georgia endured the job for a year; but after contracting a severe case of measles, she could no longer tolerate the strain on her eyes from the detailed work.

Georgia returned to Williamsburg in the fall of 1909. In a cruel twist of fate, Ida O'Keeffe had been struck with tuberculosis. In attempting to escape Wisconsin, where the illness had killed his two brothers, Frank O'Keeffe had brought his family to the damp, humid climate of Williamsburg and built a home of concrete blocks, creating a dark, dank environment, made to order for tuberculosis bacilli.

The dreaded lung disease, known also as consumption, plagued the United States at the beginning of the twentieth century. It was highly contagious, and the family wondered if Ida had caught it while nursing Frank's brother Bernard. There was no effective medication; the only treatment was to live at a high altitude in an area offering a warm, dry climate, which by decreasing humidity would postpone the ravages of the disease.

The O'Keeffes hoped that the mountains near Charlottesville, Virginia, might provide a remedy, so Ida and her daughters moved there and rented a modest home on Wertland Street while Frank stayed behind to sell the Williamsburg house. Once again, Ida took in college students as boarders to pay the rent. Because tuberculosis was contagious, the O'Keeffes kept Ida's illness a secret. If anyone learned about the disease, the family would not be allowed to take in boarders. Despite the health risk to the students, the O'Keeffes desperately needed the extra income generated from boarding the young college men.

Becoming a Teacher

Georgia still longed to be an artist, but that dream seemed to grow more remote every day. Her mother needed her help at home, but more importantly, the chances of a woman becoming a successful artist were slim. The art world was still almost exclusively male. A generation earlier, Mary Cassatt, an American Impressionist, had become the only female painter to achieve serious recognition. Cassatt's wealthy family had been able to support her studies in Europe. Most female American artists in Georgia's era contented themselves with becoming art teachers. When Eugene Speicher had taunted Georgia about merely being a schoolmarm artist, he was alluding to the highest status an American female artist was likely to attain. Georgia wanted more for herself, but her goals seemed unreachable.

In the spring of 1911 Elizabeth Mae Willis, the principal at Chatham, asked Georgia to fill in as a teacher for six weeks. Georgia reluctantly agreed. She had resented taking direction from many of her own art teachers, and she did not like the idea of telling students how to shape their creative endeavors.

At Chatham she was surprised to find that she enjoyed teaching. The students liked her kind, encouraging approach. For the first time, she began to think seriously about a career as an instructor. When she returned home, she had made up her mind to become a teacher.

4 "A Thing of Your Own"

Georgia returned to her family in Charlottesville in June 1911 to chart the course for her future. If she wanted to become an art teacher, she would have to earn teaching credentials. Uncertain about which college to attend, she planned to spend the summer inquiring about teacher training programs in art.

Arriving at the Wertland Street home, Georgia discovered that her father had rejoined the family. After selling the house in Williamsburg, Frank had opened a creamery in Charlottesville, making it more important than ever to conceal Ida's tuberculosis. If the public health department had learned of her illness, Frank would not have been allowed to operate the creamery.

Ida's illness was still in the early stages, and she continued to take in a few college boarders. The little money Ida earned from the students enabled her to enroll Georgia's younger sisters Ida and Anita in a six-week teacher training course at the University of Virginia.

Although Georgia admired her twenty-one-year-old sister Anita, who radiated enthusiasm and creativity, she was skeptical when Anita raved about a drawing class at the university. Georgia had formed negative opinions about most art instruction because she felt that students were taught

Anita O'Keeffe (pictured) convinced Georgia to attend her art class at the Columbia University Teachers College in New York. At first skeptical, Georgia immediately enrolled after taking one class.

with rigid methods that inhibited natural creativity and talent. However, Anita persuaded Georgia to accompany her to the class.

Georgia and Anita were seated in the classroom when Alon Bement, the thirty-seven-year-old art instructor, entered. Bement, an assistant professor of fine arts at the Columbia University Teachers College in New York, captured his students' imaginations by using sweeping hand gestures and dramatics.

Bement was an associate of Arthur Wesley Dow, head of the Department of Fine Arts at Columbia. Dow, who had gained recognition for teaching art in a way that nurtured individual creativity, stressed the importance of composition rather than mere imitation of details. Arthur Young, Bement's associate at the University of Virginia, explained Dow's method. "It was a freeing device so that you didn't have to draw feet, elbows or ankles."[45] Instead, Dow taught students to focus on filling a space with a balanced, pleasing composition. Dow stressed that the artist should select and emphasize certain aspects of a composition—in direct opposition to more traditional instruction, which dictated the creation of a realistic image. These fundamental beliefs were the very tenets Georgia had always embraced. Later she described the revelation she experienced in Bement's class: "Art could be a thing of your own."[46]

Suddenly Georgia realized that art could be taught effectively without boring, rigid exercises. Dow's methods seemed to be "equipment to work with."[47]

A New Vision

Georgia rushed to the registrar's office and enrolled in Bement's most advanced class, Drawing IV. Although the summer session had already begun, she had missed only a few sessions. She paid for the course with her earnings from teaching at Chatham.

For six weeks, Bement's classes met each weekday in the late summer afternoons. Georgia learned a great deal, and she also liked Bement's hands-off style. He introduced ideas to the class, then allowed his students to assimilate and adapt the information in their own way. Later, Georgia jokingly summarized Bement's method. "I had a teacher who was very good because he didn't know anything. He would just tell me things to see and to read. . . . And he'd tell me things that I should do but I never paid any attention to that."[48]

However, Georgia acknowledged that Bement actually taught her a great deal. Using Dow's text, *The Theory and Practice of Teaching Art*, Bement introduced Georgia to the author's exercises, which included dividing a square, working within a circle, and enclosing a drawing with a rectangle. Students were then instructed to balance a composition by adding or eliminating elements and changing the placement of masses. Bement was immediately impressed with his new student. He recognized her unique talents and admired her quick intellect.

During the summer session, Georgia received a letter from a friend informing her of a job opening for an art teacher in Amarillo, Texas. As a child, Georgia and her older brother, Francis, had loved to listen to their mother read stories about Billy the Kid, Kit Carson, and the Wild West. Georgia had always been intrigued by the thought of the wide, flat open plains of Texas, and she decided to apply for the position. Although she lacked the necessary credentials, Alon Bement wrote Georgia glowing recommendations. When Georgia learned that she had been selected for the teaching job, she was elated.

Georgia immediately fell in love with Texas. Later, she described her feeling toward the open plains. "This was my country, terrible winds and wonderful emptiness."[49]

A New Age in American Art

In 1913 the American art world was shaken by an exhibit of modern works known as the Armory Show because it was held at the 69th Street Armory in New York City. The early examples of modernism exhibited changed the direction of American art. In a catalog written in 1963 for the Rose Art Museum of Brandeis University, Sam Hunter explained the significance of this new phase of American expression.

"Once the collective nature of our modernism is established, and its character as a movement has been accepted, one can pick out more readily the threads of identifiable originality that separate American and European expression. The evidence of originality in the continuing dialogue with European authority interestingly provides a link between the modernism of the Armory Show period and contemporary abstraction. . . . The tradition of biomorphic [painted shapes of organic forms] abstraction, on the other hand, was given a very individual inflection by Dove and O'Keeffe. O'Keeffe in particular seemed able to invest abstract painting with new content, and significant new forms. . . . Despite their essential modesty of scale and ambition, and without being an actual influence, the paintings of O'Keeffe and Dove prefigure attitudes and an imagery that belong to contemporary abstraction; they are part of an intelligible continuity of taste and change. Firmly rooted in European precedent and innovation, they nevertheless contribute significantly to the emerging definition of a new American abstraction."

Teaching in Texas

As Georgia matured, she had come to find enclosed spaces covered with greenery to be suffocating. Unsurprisingly, then, she loved to walk out on the plains surrounding Amarillo at dawn, energized by the bleak vista meeting the changing sky. Returning at night when the stars and moon illuminated the flat land, she felt a new kinship with nature that touched her profoundly. Not since her youth in Wisconsin had she felt so free.

Georgia loved teaching, and she discovered Dow's exercises to be very effective. She began one exercise by having students draw a door inside a square. Then she urged them to think about the composition before adding other elements: "Anything to start them thinking about how to divide a space."[50] For another lesson, Georgia had her family send an array of autumn leaves from Virginia for her students to examine.

Although Georgia liked many aspects of teaching and living in Amarillo, the town that Georgia discovered upon her

Georgia O'Keeffe at the time she taught art in Amarillo, Texas. O'Keeffe loved mixing with the cowboys that populated the town after cattle drives. While Georgia pursued her career, her younger sister Ida (right) remained at home to take care of their mother.

arrival in August 1912 differed greatly from the romantic vision created by her mother's readings long ago. A major railroad depot, Amarillo was used as a holding place for thousands of long-horned cattle. The cattle were kept in cramped, fenced stockyards before being loaded in railway cars for shipment to Chicago. The smell from the holding pens often hung over the town, and every night the cries of the cattle permeated Georgia's room at the Magnolia Hotel on Polk Street. Biographer Laurie Lisle described this Amarillo institution:

> The Magnolia's dining room was popular with the ravenous cowboys fresh from the cattle drives whose lips were blistered by the sun and eyes were bloodshot from the wind. Georgia watched with amazement as they wolfed down two or three complete dinners in

one sitting. Hard drinkers, oldtimers, loose women, and card sharks also frequented the hotel, and she heard vivid talk about outlaws, cattle rustlers, and violent frontier justice.[51]

While the other young teachers stayed in boardinghouses, Georgia preferred living in the hotel so that she could mingle with the cowboys and other characters drifting through the town. Georgia dined with these men and spent her evenings playing dominoes with the other guests, but she found most of them to be surprisingly crude and incapable of sustaining a meaningful conversation.

The citizens of Amarillo found Georgia strange. Although the cultures of Virginia and Texas differed greatly, people in both regions expected a young woman to conform to certain codes of dress and behavior. Not only did Georgia dress in a way the people found odd, she had no friends and continued her habit of taking long walks alone. As one student described the young art teacher, "I never saw her in anything except tailored suits and oxfords that were square-toed. . . . Her hair was cut just like a man's, short. . . . She wore a man's type felt hat."[52]

In June 1913 Georgia returned to Charlottesville, where she served as Bement's assistant at the university. The O'Keeffe household was rapidly changing.

Memories of Amarillo, Texas

Georgia held a romantic vision of Texas, based on her mother's readings when Georgia was a child. When she accepted a teaching position in Amarillo in 1912, she found a place that differed from her childish imagination. She recalled those impressions in her autobiography.

"Texas had always been a sort of far-away dream. When we were children my mother read to us every evening and on Sunday afternoons. It was particularly for my older brother, whose eyes were not very good. I had listened for many hours to boys' stories—Stanley's adventures in Africa, Hannibal crossing the Alps, Julius Caesar, 'Pilgrim's Progress,' all the Leatherstocking tales, stories of the Wild West of Texas, Kit Carson and Billy the Kid. It had always seemed to me that the West must be wonderful—there was no place I knew of that I would rather go—so when I had a chance to teach there—off I went to Texas—not knowing much about teaching.

Amarillo, Texas, was the cattle-shipping center for a large area of the Southwest. Trains ran east and west and north and south. For days we would see large herds of cattle with their clouds of dust being driven slowly across the plains toward the town. When the cattle arrived they were put in pens near the station, separated from their calves and sometimes kept there for 2 or 3 days—particularly haunting at night.

From the Plains I and *Orange and Red Streak* were painted months after I left that wide world. And years later, I painted it twice again. The cattle in the pens lowing for their calves day and night was a sound that has always haunted me. It has a regular rhythmic beat like the old Penitente [a Catholic religious society in New Mexico] songs, repeating the same rhythms over and over all through the day and night. It was loud and raw under the stars and that wide empty country."

Georgia's brothers no longer lived at home. Francis was away studying to become an architect, and Alexis attended engineering school. Georgia's sister Ida had become a pillar in the O'Keeffe home, helping her mother and looking after the younger girls.

Following her second year in Amarillo, Georgia learned that Texas was adopting art texts to be used in all the schools in the state, beginning in the fall of 1914. This move went against everything that Georgia believed in. Refusing to be bound by rigid, prescribed methods, which she characterized as death, she vowed to fight the decision. However, Georgia had no allies. She had forged no friendships in Amarillo, and no one else supported her convictions. In frustration, Georgia resigned and returned to Charlottesville.

Back in Virginia

Georgia was shocked at the conditions she found in the family home. Frank O'Keeffe had sold the creamery and had taken a job as a state construction supervisor, necessitating long trips out of town. Increasingly depressed about finances and concerned about his wife's worsening health, he seemed to prefer life on the road. Now too ill to cook for boarders, Ida rented a room to a young couple, and this seemed to be her primary source of income.

Ida O'Keeffe had always held the family together, even in the worst of times. While she never expressed regrets over giving up her plans to become a doctor when she married Frank O'Keeffe, she constantly encouraged her children to pursue an education. As the family's cir-

cumstances steadily declined, she made sure every available penny went toward tuition for her children at the best schools the O'Keeffes could afford.

The O'Keeffe children had been largely shielded from the seriousness of the family's declining fortunes. For many years, Ida had gone about the running of the household, maintaining a serene, optimistic outlook and assuring her children that the future would be better. Ironically, in teaching her children to be strong and independent, Ida had also stressed the need to place a premium on personal ambition. Consequently, even when tuberculosis struck Ida, her children put their own plans for the future ahead of helping their mother.

When the news of the family's plight reached Georgia's Aunt Ollie in Chicago, she responded by sending Georgia a year's tuition for the Columbia Teachers College in New York City. Georgia was delighted at the prospect of studying under Arthur Dow. As she assisted Alon Bement at the University of Virginia, she could hardly wait to return to New York. Assured that her mother was being looked after, Georgia left for New York in September.

In the fall of 1914 Georgia found an invigorated art world in New York. A highly controversial art show held the year before in New York's 69th Regiment Armory had ignited a great debate about accepted artistic expression. The Armory Show ushered in a new era, breaking with strictly classical art and paving the road for modernism. Georgia felt the atmosphere of excitement and was glad to be part of it.

Georgia found a modest room near the university, on the upper west side of Manhattan. With no extra money, she decorated her small four-dollar-a-month room in the spartan style that would later become her trademark. The room featured white walls and held only a few pieces of furniture. She covered her bed with unbleached muslin and draped matching fabric over the window. The only decoration was a small pot of red geraniums resting on the fire escape outside her window.

Similarly, her style of dress was simple. A friend later observed that because Georgia dressed so smartly, no one suspected she had so little money. At Sacred Heart, the nuns had taught her to sew, and although she could afford only a few outfits, she always looked stylish, fashioning her clothing from the finest dark-colored fabrics. Her shirtwaists (blouses) were always clean, starched, and pressed. During this time, she began to dress entirely in black, and this too became an O'Keeffe trademark.

Georgia enrolled as a candidate for the bachelor of science degree in fine arts education at Columbia. There, she met Anita Pollitzer, also a fine arts education major, and the two women forged a lasting friendship. Many years later, Pollitzer remembered her initial impressions of her friend. "There was something insatiable about her, as direct as an arrow, and completely independent."[53]

New York's Art World

Anita and Georgia reveled in New York's stimulating art world, where they attended exhibits and met many influential new artists. They frequently stopped at Alfred Stieglitz's 291 Gallery. During one visit, they saw an exhilarating show entitled *Younger American Painters in Paris.* Georgia

After O'Keeffe enrolled at Columbia, she met fellow art student Anita Pollitzer (pictured). The two became lifelong friends.

was struck by an abstract painting called *Leaf Forms,* by Arthur Dove, whose pure abstract style closely paralleled her own.

That semester Georgia finally met Arthur Wesley Dow. Although she had been impressed by his text on art instruction and had embraced his teachings, she found him disappointingly meek. Conversely, Dow described Georgia as "one of the most talented people in art that we have ever had."[54]

Although Georgia was a favorite in her art classes, her first-semester grade report reveals a characteristic lack of interest in other subjects. With two years of teaching experience under her belt, she was bored with instructional methods. She earned a C in a course on the principles of teaching and a D in English.

In June 1915 Georgia returned to Charlottesville to assist Alon Bement once again. She also continued to paint that summer and for the first time began to share her paintings. Since her earliest days as an artist, Georgia had preferred to destroy her works rather than give them away. Envisioning herself as an artist with a great future, she feared that one day her crude, early works would surface to embarrass her. It was also difficult for Georgia to give away her art; it was as if she were giving away a piece of her soul. However, her new friendship with Anita Pollitzer forged a bond and a trust Georgia had never experienced, and she began to send her works to her friend in New York.

But Georgia also harbored ambivalence about parting with her works. While she hoped that Anita might share them

"One of the Best Times of My Life"

In her autobiography, Georgia O'Keeffe, *the author recalled the artistic rebirth that she experienced in Columbia, South Carolina, in 1915.*

"It was in the fall of 1915 that I first had the idea that what I had been taught was of little value to me except for the use of materials as a language—charcoal, pencil, pen and ink, watercolor, pastel, and oil. I had become fluent with them when I was so young that they were simply another language that I had handled easily. But what to say with them? I had been taught to work like others and after careful thinking I decided that I wasn't going to spend my life doing what had already been done.

I hung on the wall the work I had been doing for several months. Then I sat down and looked at it. I could see how each painting or drawing had been done according to one teacher or another, and I said to myself, 'I have things in my head that are not like what anyone has taught me—shapes and ideas so near to me—so natural to my way of being and thinking that it hasn't occurred to me to put them down.' I decided to start anew—to strip away what I had been taught—to accept as true my own thinking. This was one of the best times of my life. There was no one around to look at what I was doing—no one interested—no one to say anything about it one way or another. I was alone and singularly free, working into my own, unknown—no one to satisfy but myself. I began with charcoal and paper and decided not to use any color until it was impossible to do what I wanted to do in black and white."

with an influential individual in New York's art circles such as Alfred Stieglitz, she also dreaded the thought. She expressed those sentiments in another letter to Pollitzer:

> I feel bothered about that stuff I sent. . . . I wish I hadn't sent it. I always have a curious sort of feeling about some of my things—I hate to show them—I am perfectly inconsistent about it—I am afraid people won't understand—and I hope they won't—and I am afraid they will . . . they are at your mercy—do as you please with them.[55]

Georgia planned to resume her studies in New York in September, but she had depleted Aunt Ollie's financial gift. She refused to apply for a scholarship, which she considered charity. Realizing that returning to college was an impossibility, she reluctantly accepted a teaching position in Columbia, South Carolina.

Teaching College in South Carolina

In September 1915 Georgia began teaching at Columbia College, a Methodist school for women just outside the South Carolina capital. She disliked the school and the community. The religious character of the school combined with South Carolina's humidity to produce an atmosphere that Georgia found oppressive.

"I feel all sick inside," she wrote Anita Pollitzer, "as if I could dry up and blow away right now."[56] The college's primary mission was to train music teachers, but its enrollment had declined to just three hundred students and the school was ex-periencing severe financial problems. Georgia had been selected for the position because the school could pay her a meager salary on the grounds that she lacked proper teaching credentials.

A growing feeling of isolation consumed Georgia. Her steady correspondence with Pollitzer helped her through this bleak period. Although she had not played music for many years, she suddenly found consolation in the violin. And, as always, she had her art.

In addition to painting, Georgia had much time to think about art. A nagging theme continued to plague her and once again she asked herself the fundamental question: Was she painting for herself or was she still trying to impress others? In the summer of 1915, she had written to Anita:

> I believe I would rather have Stieglitz like something—anything I had done—than anyone else I know of—I have always felt that—If I ever make anything that satisfies me ever so little—I am going to show it to him to find out if it is any good. Don't you often wish you could make something he would like?[57]

But, showing her ambivalence about this desire to impress Stieglitz, Georgia had added, "I don't know why we ever think of what others think of what we do—no matter who they are—isn't it enough just to express yourself?"[58]

An Artistic Rebirth

Georgia's late twenties were a period of profound growth and reflection. Suddenly, she found her earlier works repulsive. "I

Charcoal Drawings of 1915–1916

In Georgia O'Keeffe, *Lisa Mintz Messinger discusses O'Keeffe's early drawings and the impact the instructor Arthur Wesley Dow had on O'Keeffe the artist.*

"In O'Keeffe's early charcoal drawings and watercolors of 1915–16 we witness her breakthrough from the academic training that she received toward modern abstraction. In South Carolina during the fall of 1915 she first began to draw simple, abstract forms from her imagination that expressed her feelings and experiences. To permit the full exploration of these forms O'Keeffe eliminated the distraction of color, working exclusively with black charcoal applied to large white sheets of paper.

O'Keeffe began these charcoal drawings only a few months after studying with Arthur Wesley Dow at Teachers College, and his influence is strongly felt in her first independent work. . . . Dow taught that through the artist's selective orchestration of format and compositional elements (line, shape, color, and value) each subject's true identity could be revealed. Harmony and balance were the key words in his theories. O'Keeffe absorbed Dow's lessons well, and throughout her career she produced primarily serene images of nature that relied on her sensitive arrangement of elements for their emotive power. In the 1915–16 drawings, she seems to have adopted many of the vegetal shapes and graphic patterns found in Dow's own representational work and in the illustrations to his book *Composition* (1914).

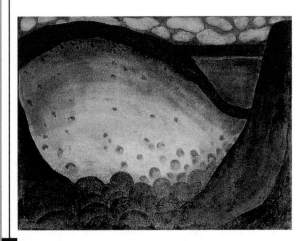

Where O'Keeffe asserted her personal vision was in her application of these design concepts and visual motifs to an abstract idiom. . . . Moreover, the 1915–16 drawings exude a sense of vital energy and movement that was never an issue in Dow's theories."

One of O'Keeffe's early charcoal drawings, Special No. 15. *The drawings would astound both Anita Pollitzer and Alfred Stieglitz.*

Georgia's insistence on beginning again—putting away her paints and working only with charcoal— led her to develop her impressive and unique style. Pictured is another early charcoal, Early #2.

as if, at age twenty-seven, she was starting over. Georgia later told an interviewer that it was like learning to walk all over again. Crawling on her hands and knees, she worked furiously, producing powerfully stark abstract charcoal sketches.

Georgia worked feverishly at night for weeks until she had exhausted her vigorous creative energies. She had undergone a rebirth. A new woman and a new artist had emerged. Recalling this period, she wrote:

> I grew up pretty much as everybody else grows up and one day seven years ago found myself saying to myself—I can't live where I want to—I can't go where I want to—I can't even say what I want to. School and things that painters have taught me even keep me from painting as I want to. I decided I was a very stupid fool not to at least paint as I wanted to when I painted as that seemed to be the only thing I could do that didn't concern anybody but myself—that was nobody's business but my own. So these paintings and drawings happened and many other things with color and shapes that I couldn't say in any other way— things that I had no words for.[60]

At last, Georgia O'Keeffe had given free rein to her inner voice. In doing so, she had also given birth to a body of work that would speak to the American art world.

feel disgusted and I am glad I am disgusted," she wrote to Anita.[59] Filled with the images of things she wanted to draw, she put away her watercolors. She pared down her materials to the barest essentials. Each night she stretched rough student sketch paper across the floor. It was

5 "A Woman on Paper"

Anita Pollitzer sat in her room on January 1, 1916. She held a package that had just arrived from her friend Georgia O'Keeffe in South Carolina. When she opened the parcel, she discovered a roll of charcoal drawings. As she unrolled the sketches, she was immediately moved by the power

After receiving charcoal drawings from O'Keeffe, Anita Pollitzer immediately wrapped them back up and took them to Stieglitz. Pictured is Special #12.

of the collection. "I was struck by their aliveness," Pollitzer later said. "They were different. Here were charcoals on the same kind of paper that all art students were using, and through no trick, no superiority of tools, these drawings were saying what had not yet been said."[61]

O'Keeffe had sent her friend the series of sketches she had recently completed in Columbia, asking Pollitzer to show them at the university but secretly hoping that they would be shared with Alfred Stieglitz.

That afternoon Pollitzer tucked the roll of sketches under her arm and went to a matinee at a local theater. Coming out into the rain after the show, she headed for Stieglitz's gallery at 291 Fifth Avenue. Many young art students were intimidated by the famous photographer's gruff manner, but the confident Pollitzer enjoyed a good rapport with him. She respected Stieglitz and found him to be the most dynamic figure in New York's art world.

The American painter Marsden Hartley recalled Pollitzer's objectives in sharing Georgia O'Keeffe's work with Stieglitz:

The lively little woman's argument was that having looked at the drawings, deriving singular sensations and experiences from them, and felt that despite their author's admonitions—these

Stieglitz Discovers O'Keeffe's Work

In late December 1915, O'Keeffe sent sketches she had completed in South Carolina to her friend Anita Pollitzer in New York. Pollitzer was so impressed that she immediately took them to Stieglitz at Gallery 291. The same night in a letter she informed her friend of Stieglitz's reaction. O'Keeffe responded to the news by return mail. The letters excerpted here are from A Woman on Paper, *Pollitzer's biography of O'Keeffe.*

"Astounded and awfully happy were my feelings today when I opened the batch of drawings. I tell you I felt them! & when I say that I mean that. They've gotten past the personal stage into the big sort of emotions that are common to big people—but it's your version of it. . . . Stieglitz said. 'Are you writing to this girl soon?' I said 'Yes'—'Well tell her,' he said 'They're the purest, fairest, sincerest things that have entered 291 in a long while'—and he said—'I wouldn't mind showing them in one of these rooms one bit—perhaps I shall.'"

"Columbia, South Carolina, January 4, 1916

There seems to be nothing for me to say except Thank you—very calmly and quietly. I could hardly believe my eyes when I read your letter this afternoon—I haven't been working—except one night—all during the holidays—that night I worked till nearly morning—The thing seems to express in a way what I want it to but—it also seems rather effeminate—it is essentially a woman's feeling—satisfies me in a way. . . . Of course marks on a paper are free—free speech-press-pictures—all go together I suppose—but I was feeling rather downcast about it—and it is so nice to feel that I said something to you—and to Stieglitz.

Anyway, Anita—it makes me want to keep on—and I had almost rather decided that it was fool's game—Of course I would rather have something hang in 291 than any place in New York—but wanting things hung is simply wanting your vanity satisfied—of course it sounds good but what sounds best to me is that he liked them."

drawings should be shown to someone closer to these ideas than she could lay claim to be—that is to say—she felt they must have consideration from someone more actually related to esthetic interests, and so she brought them to that unusual little room—two-ninety-one.[62]

She climbed the four flights of stairs to Stieglitz's gallery. She found him alone,

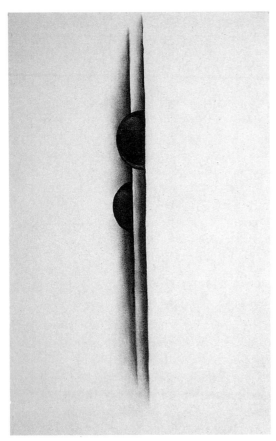

Stieglitz agreed with Pollitzer's assessment of O'Keeffe's charcoals. He sponsored the charcoals in the first public display of O'Keeffe's work. Pictured is Special #39.

weary after a day of visitors. As always, he appeared disheveled, his hair mussed, his expensive suit hanging on his short frame. Pollitzer spread the sketches out on the bare floor. Stieglitz carefully examined each one in what seemed like an eternity of silence. Finally he spoke: "At last, a woman on paper."[63] Stieglitz realized that the work of a woman destined for fame lay before him. Behind tiny spectacles, his dark eyes revealed his great excitement.

He asked Pollitzer to tell the artist that her drawings were the "purest, finest, sin-

cerest things that have entered 291 in a long while."[64] Stieglitz exhibited them in May 1916 along with the work of two others. It was the first public display of the art of Georgia O'Keeffe.

Pollitzer raced back to her room and dashed off a letter, informing her friend about Stieglitz's reaction. Thrilled, O'Keeffe immediately began corresponding with the photographer. The two came to know each other through many letters traveling between New York and South Carolina.

Returning to New York to Columbia University

Despite the exciting work she had produced in Columbia, O'Keeffe remained frustrated with the college and surprised the administration by suddenly resigning soon after the start of the second semester. Officials at the West Texas Normal (teacher training) School had contacted her about a position, but they wanted her to complete Arthur Wesley Dow's teaching methods course at Columbia University. She jumped at the chance to return to New York.

Arriving in New York in early March, O'Keeffe started Professor Dow's class several weeks late. She stayed with Anita Pollitzer's aunt and uncle, occupying their spare bedroom and eating meals at the university. She was happy to be reunited with her friends at Columbia, but her joy was short-lived.

On May 2, 1916, the landlady appeared at the O'Keeffes' Wertland Avenue home in Charlottesville, demanding the overdue rent. Georgia's sisters Ida and

Catherine explained that they had no money and their father was not at home. They said that their mother was extremely ill and confined to bed. When the irate landlady demanded to see Mrs. O'Keeffe, the frightened young women went upstairs to inform their mother. Ida was gravely ill, her frail body ravaged by tuberculosis, but she insisted on talking to the landlady. She rose from her bed, and then, as her daughters helped her down the hall, Ida O'Keeffe collapsed and died.

When Georgia learned of her mother's death, she took an overnight train to Virginia. Arriving at the family home, she learned that no one there had seen Frank O'Keeffe for months. There was not a crumb of food in the house;

"The Visual Effect of Emotions"

Critics saw various elements in O'Keeffe's first charcoal sketches. William Murrell Fisher reviewed O'Keeffe's first solo exhibit at 291 in Camera Work. *This excerpt is taken from* Georgia O'Keeffe: An Exhibition of the Work of the Artist from 1915 to 1966, *edited by Mitchell A. Wilder.*

"In recent years there have been many deliberate attempts to translate into line and color the visual effect of emotions aroused by music, and I am inclined to think they failed just because they were so deliberate. The setting down of such purely mental forms escapes the conscious hand—one must become, as it were, a channel, a willing medium, through which the visible music flows. And doubtless it more often comes from unheard melodies than from the listening to instruments—from the true music of the spheres referred to by the mystics of all ages. Quite sensibly, there is an inner law of harmony at work in the composition of these drawings and paintings by Miss O'Keeffe, and they are more truly inspired than any work I have seen; and although, as is frequently the case with 'given writings' and religious 'revelation' most are but fragments of vision, incompleted movements, yet even the effect is of a quite cosmic grandeur. Of all things earthly, it is only in music that one finds any analogy to the emotional content of these drawings—to the gigantic, swirling rhythms, and the exquisite tenderness so powerfully and sensitively rendered—and music is the condition towards which, according to [critic Walter] Pater, all art constantly aspires. Well, plastic art, in the hands of Miss O'Keeffe, seems now to have approximated that."

apparently there had been little to eat for weeks. With no money for food, Georgia's sisters had been shooting squirrels and existing on their meat. Horrified at the conditions her mother and sisters had endured, Georgia was consumed by grief and guilt.

As the weeks passed following Ida O'Keeffe's death, Georgia once again resumed her summer job teaching at the University of Virginia as Bement's assistant. Deeply depressed, she found painting a means of expressing her profound grief. Usually she preferred oil paints and bright colors such as red, but that summer she painted mostly watercolors and used primarily blue tones. Among the works created in O'Keeffe's *Blue Series* were two compositions featuring simple lines, a near-abstract *Tent Door at Night* and *Blue Lines.*

Teaching in Texas Again

Georgia left Charlottesville in September 1916 to begin teaching in Canyon, Texas, just south of Amarillo. Her youngest sister, Claudia, went with her and enrolled in the school where Georgia taught. It was a new beginning for both women.

Primarily an agricultural community, and smaller than Amarillo, Canyon was enjoying economic prosperity. The West Texas Normal School was housed in a brand-new building, and new private homes were springing up everywhere. Georgia rented a room with a family. Although she had a magnificent view of the plains, she hated her room with its silver-and-white-striped wallpaper and white furniture. To add her own touch, she framed a piece of black cloth and hung it on the wall.

O'Keeffe became a true Texan, adopting many of the local customs. She took long walks, giving neighbors the impression that she could outwalk any man in Canyon. To relax, she often shot tin cans on the outskirts of town. "I got a box of bullets and went out on the plains and threw [tin cans] into the air and shot them. It's a great sport."[65]

But no matter how much she adopted the ways of Texans, the townspeople still found her an oddity. One citizen of Canyon later described her: "Oh, she wore black. Black, black, black! And her clothing was all like men's clothing. Straight lines, she didn't believe in lace, or jabots

West Texas Normal School in Canyon, Texas, where O'Keeffe taught following the death of her mother.

The art room at West Texas Normal School. On the wall are teaching aids that O'Keeffe hung to inspire her students. Included are pictures of Greek pottery, textiles, and Persian plates.

in blouses, laces, or ruffles or things like that. Everything on straight lines."[66]

Indeed, Georgia O'Keeffe did like straight lines. She reveled in the flatness of the land extending as far as the eye could see. She used watercolors to capture the stark beauty she saw. "The whole sky— and there is so much of it out here—was just blazing," she remarked. "And gray-blue clouds were rioting all through the hotness of it."[67] Drawn to the magnificent sandstone formations jutting out from the plains, she produced a series of Palo Duro Canyon landscape scenes that became known as *Specials*.

O'Keeffe enjoyed teaching. She used her creative eye to search out objects in the natural environment for her students to draw. She was fascinated by the smooth, pristine bones of animals that she found on the plains, bleached pure white by the sun. Their varying sizes and shapes became an important theme in her work. A student later described the land, its treasures, and how her teacher used both.

You know, this was open country . . . sometimes when there were large herds brought in around town some cattle would die . . . and just lie there and bleach out. I remember [O'Keeffe] brought a skull in and large leg bones and told us how beautiful they were— the sheen on those dried bones, and the look of the bones.[68]

Inspired, O'Keeffe began to paint the scenes around Palo Duro Canyon where steam rose above orange foam from boiling underground springs. O'Keeffe thought in color the way others think in words. She also had acute depth perception.

Vernon Hunter, an artist of the Southwest, discussed the impact of Canyon, Texas, on the art of Georgia O'Keeffe:

And "this country" being a region of great areas, almost horizontal with the slowest and most fluent of earth curves which are lyrical yet strong because of the size but not violent because of the almost passive horizontality, might seem to have contributed largely to the inner structure of Miss O'Keeffe's paintings. Was it in "this country" where she walked over the plains that she, in doing so, struck a stride in her creative work? Although born in Wisconsin she may have been reborn on these great staked-plains.[69]

The sandstone formations of Palo Duro Canyon that inspired O'Keeffe's work while she taught in Canyon, Texas.

Stieglitz Exhibits O'Keeffe's Work

O'Keeffe sent her paintings to Alfred Stieglitz and continued to correspond with him. Intrigued by her intelligence and her remarkable talent, he asked her permission to exhibit more of her works at 291 and she consented. On April 3, 1917, Stieglitz opened the first show devoted completely to O'Keeffe's works. The exhibit featured the blue watercolor series and her Palo Duro landscapes. The United States entered World War I on April 6, and attention quickly turned away from the world of art, but on May 4 a prestigious newspaper, the *Christian Science Monitor*, published a review that included an observation about the artist's "female message. . . . Now perhaps for the first time in art's history, the style is the woman."[70]

The second semester at the West Texas Normal School ended in late May. There was a three-week break before the start of the summer semester, and O'Keeffe longed to see her exhibit at 291. She felt the idea of simply hopping a train for New York to be frivolous, so one Sunday afternoon she sought Claudia's advice. "If I felt as you do about it," counseled her younger sister, "I'd go."[71] Although it was Sunday, the painter went straight to the home of the bank manager, asking him to open the bank so she could withdraw some money. She purchased a train ticket and left for New York the following morning.

When O'Keeffe walked into Gallery 291 she found the walls bare. Her show had been taken down. Stieglitz had learned that the brownstone building housing the gallery would be torn down. That news, coupled with the outbreak of war, led to his decision to close the gallery. The O'Keeffe exhibit was Stieglitz's first and last one-woman show.

During her stay in New York, O'Keeffe met one of Stieglitz's followers, a brilliant young photographer named Paul Strand. He and O'Keeffe realized that their artistic styles were closely parallel: Both artists selected ordinary objects as a focus for their work, then attempted to transform what they saw into abstract form.

Stieglitz photographed O'Keeffe for the first time during her brief visit. She later described those early photographs:

Stieglitz photographed me first at his gallery "291" in the spring of 1917. I had gone all the way from Texas by train just to be there for three days and see the second show of my drawings and watercolors. I was teaching at the West Texas Normal School. A few weeks after I returned to Texas, photographs of me came—two portraits of my face against one of my large watercolors and three photographs of hands. In my excitement at such pictures of myself I took them to school and held them up for my class to see. They were surprised and astonished too. Nothing like that had come into our world before.[72]

In the warm Texas evenings, she walked out on the plains alone to paint the evening star, producing a striking series called *Evening Star*. Georgia's fellow teachers found her abstract treatments strange, but she was accustomed to such criticism and she ignored it.

In August Georgia and Claudia traveled to Colorado and New Mexico. It was Georgia's first exposure to New Mexico

First Solo Show

On April 3, 1917, the first solo exhibit of Georgia O'Keeffe's work opened at Alfred Stieglitz's gallery in New York City. On May 4 the Christian Science Monitor *published this review by Henry Tyrell, who observed Georgia's "female message." It is quoted by Roxana Robinson in* Georgia O'Keeffe: A Life.

"The recent work . . . of Miss Georgia O'Keeffe of Canyon, Texas . . . has to speak for itself as it is not numbered, catalogued, labeled, lettered or identified in any way—in fact, it is not even signed. The interesting but little-known personality of the artist . . . is perhaps the only real key, and even that would not open all the chambers of the haunted palace which is a gifted woman's heart. . . . [She] has found expression in delicately veiled symbolism for 'what every woman knows,' but what women heretofore kept to themselves . . . the loneliness and privation which her emotional nature must have suffered put their impress on everything she does. Her strange art affects people variously and some, not at all . . . artists especially wonder at its technical resourcefulness for dealing with what hitherto has been deemed the inexpressible—in visual form, at least. . . . Now perhaps for the first time in art's history, the style is the woman."

and the beauty of the land burned into her soul. "From then on," she later said, "I was always on my way back."[73]

O'Keeffe and Stieglitz

In December 1917 Claudia O'Keeffe accepted a teaching position in Spur, Texas, leaving thirty-year-old Georgia alone for the first time in over a year. She filled the lonely hours with her work and continued sending paintings to Stieglitz, who encouraged her efforts. She also found much comfort in her correspondence with the man who was twenty-five years her elder. She respected his opinions and admired

One of Stieglitz's early photos of O'Keeffe. Stieglitz would continue to photograph the artist throughout her life. These photos became some of Stieglitz's most well known.

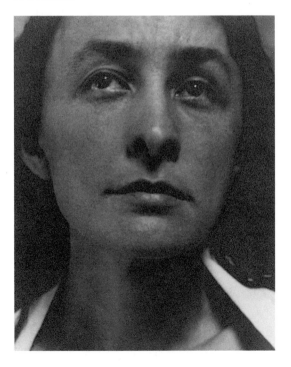

his insight into art and life. Although Stieglitz was married, he and his wife, Emmy, had been unhappy for years. Stieglitz had moved out of the home and was living in a studio. He was very fond of O'Keeffe, and their friendship evolved into love through their letters.

In January 1918 Georgia contracted a serious case of influenza. Still too ill to return to work in February, she asked the college for a medical leave of absence.

Leah Harris, another faculty member, also recovering from an illness, invited O'Keeffe to stay with her on her farm south of Canyon. One night, a prowler appeared at a window. Terrified, Harris grabbed a gun and pointed it at the man, who ran away. When O'Keeffe related the event to Stieglitz in a letter, he became concerned about her welfare.

Stieglitz contacted his younger friend Paul Strand, asking him if he would travel to Texas and escort O'Keeffe to New York. When Strand agreed, Stieglitz gave the young man money for train fare, and Strand set out for Canyon.

O'Keeffe valued her independence, but for the first time in her life she admitted that she needed help. She was deeply attracted to Stieglitz, but she was not sure whether she should return to New York with Strand. Later, she described her decision to return with Strand as "the vague intuitive way that I go at life . . . interested . . . amused . . . like or dislike . . . for no particular reason . . . excepting that it is inevitable at the moment."[74]

When the travelers arrived in New York, O'Keeffe was still feverish and coughing. Stieglitz had arranged for her to stay at his niece's unoccupied studio at 114 East 59th Street, two bright rooms with pale yellow walls. Stieglitz brought

Canyon, Texas

In her autobiography, O'Keeffe recalled the walks she and her sister took on the plains during the years she spent in Canyon, Texas.

"When I taught in Canyon, Texas, my sister Claudia was with me. Saturdays, right after breakfast, we often drove the 20 miles to the Palo Duro Canyon. It was colorful like a small Grand Canyon, but most of it only a mile wide. It was a place where few people went unless they had cattle they hoped had found shelter there in bad weather. The weather seemed to go over it. It was quiet down in the canyon. We saw the wind and snow blow across the slit in the plains as if the slit didn't exist.

The only paths were narrow winding cow paths. There was sharp, high edges between long soft earth banks so steep that you couldn't see the bottom. They made the canyon seem very deep. We took different paths from the edge so that we could climb down in new places. We sometimes had to go down together holding to a horizontal stick to keep one another from falling. . . . Often as we were leaving, we would see a long line of cattle like black lace against the sunset sky.

Those perilous climbs were frightening but it was wonderful to me and not like anything I had ever known before."

her food daily and cared for her. As O'Keeffe recovered, she grew to love the sparsely decorated studio, where she placed her bed beneath the skylights so she could look up at stars before she went to sleep. During one of Stieglitz's visits, they discussed her plans for the future. O'Keeffe remembered the conversation:

The one day he asked if I could do anything I wanted to do for a year, what would it be. I promptly said I would like to have a year to paint. I enjoyed my work teaching, but I would rather just try to paint for a year. He thought for awhile and then remarked that he thought he could arrange that—so I kept on painting in the studio.[75]

O'Keeffe felt that this was her opportunity to break into the New York art world, and she seized the chance. She had once written to Anita Pollitzer, "I'm glad I want everything in the world—good and bad—bitter and sweet—I want it all and a lot of it too."[76]

Chapter

6 Invading a Man's World

In the spring of 1918 news of the romance between Georgia O'Keeffe and Alfred Stieglitz spread throughout New York's art circles. Describing their mutual respect, O'Keeffe wrote, "The relationship was really very good because it was built on something more than just emotional needs. Each of us was really interested in what the other was doing."[77]

However, Stieglitz, still married, insisted that he was merely encouraging a young artist. His wife, Emmy, heir to her family's brewery fortune, had always financed her husband's career, but she took no interest in Stieglitz's photography. The couple had drifted apart over the years and their marriage was essentially over. But divorces were uncommon at that time, and Alfred and Emmy remained legally married.

In June Stieglitz invited O'Keeffe to accompany him to his family's summer home, Oaklawn, in Lake George, New York, where they stayed with Hedwig, his widowed mother, and numerous relatives. O'Keeffe had never seen such a gathering of relatives, or a house filled with so many furnishings and decorations. Recalling their arrival at Oaklawn, she described her initial impressions of the Stieglitz family:

O'Keeffe (holding saw) at the Stieglitz family's summer home in Lake George, New York. Once the married Stieglitz brought O'Keeffe there, their romance was no longer a secret.

The Independent Artist

It was not until O'Keeffe began to please herself in her art that she found fulfillment. The following quote is taken from a 1923 catalog of her work.

"I grew up pretty much as everybody else grows up and one day seven years ago found myself saying to myself—I can't live where I want to—I can't go where I want to—I can't do what I want to—I can't even say what I want to. School and things that painters have taught me even keep me from painting as I want to. I decided I was a very stupid fool not to at least paint as I wanted to when I painted as that seemed to be the only thing I could do that didn't concern anybody but myself—that was nobody's business but my own. So these paintings and drawings happened and many others that are not here. I found that I could say things with color and shapes that I couldn't say in any other way—things that I had no words for."

Finally, we went to the country to his mother's house. She met us at the porch steps as we were driven up to it under the trees by old Fred who had always met people at the station. Stieglitz's mother was dignified—her eyes were dark and wide. She was not tall and not thin—hair parted in the middle and done way in the back. The house was shocking to me—so very full of all kinds of things collected by a traveling family. Stieglitz I thought of as I saw him at his gallery 291—the simplest, barest of rooms, not even a chair.[78]

While O'Keeffe may have felt overwhelmed by her new surroundings, the Stieglitz family welcomed her into the fold. Even Hedwig Stieglitz rejoiced, having witnessed her son's alienation and sorrow stemming from his unhappy marriage.

Now, he seemed transformed, and it was obvious he and O'Keeffe loved each other. In a letter to his friend Paul Strand, Stieglitz wrote, "The days here are the most perfect of all my life. . . . Every moment is complete in itself and full to bursting."[79]

The pair paid a price for their happiness, however. Stieglitz's relationship with the younger woman insulted and humiliated his wife. Furious that Stieglitz had taken another woman to Lake George, she refused to divorce him. Their daughter, Kitty, deeply hurt by Stieglitz's relationship with O'Keeffe, completely rejected her father. He was in turn anguished over the estrangement from his only child.

Most of that summer was magical nevertheless. Free to relax and rest in the fresh mountain air, O'Keeffe finally recovered from the lingering effects of influenza. "After the evening meal," she wrote, "we almost always went on the lake

*Stieglitz began to take many
more photos of O'Keeffe,
especially of her hands.*

in the rowboat and watched the light fade
over the mountains and the water."[80] Both
O'Keeffe and Stieglitz worked at their re-
spective arts that summer at Lake George,
as they would continue to do for the next
decade. For the first time, Stieglitz was
able to photograph O'Keeffe frequently
during lengthy shooting sessions.

Stieglitz Photographs O'Keeffe

Stieglitz had always dreamed of photographing an individual from birth to
death. He had begun such a project with
his daughter, but Emmy had objected and
he had discontinued the project. Now,
modifying the concept, he began to photograph Georgia in countless poses, producing exquisite black-and-white close-
ups. At times, O'Keeffe appeared serious,
while in other shots she was childlike and
clownish. He photographed various parts
of her body: eyes, lips, neck, feet, and

hands. "My hands had always been admired since I was a little girl," she wrote,
"but I never thought much about it. He
wanted head and arms and hands on a pil-
low—in many different positions. I was
asked to move my hands in many different
ways—also my head—and I had to turn
this way and that."[81] As Janet Malcolm
wrote in the *New Yorker*, "the photographs
belong among O'Keeffe's works as well as
among Stieglitz's."[82]

The couple returned to New York in
the fall. Stieglitz's niece had married,
turning the studio apartment over to her
uncle and O'Keeffe. No longer receiving
funds from his wife, Stieglitz wondered
how he would support two people—he
had encouraged O'Keeffe to give up
teaching in Texas to pursue painting for a
year, so she had no income either. Stieglitz
turned to his younger brother, Leopold,
or Lee, for help. Lee generously paid the
rent for his brother, and Stieglitz was able
to borrow a thousand dollars from a
friend to cover living expenses.

The small studio apartment was quite cramped, and there were no kitchen facilities. Thus despite their lack of money, O'Keeffe and Stieglitz began a long-lasting custom of dining out every evening. With no domestic responsibilities, they devoted all their energies to their work.

Realizing that she would not be returning to Canyon, O'Keeffe sent to Texas for her belongings and art equipment. When a barrel arrived containing her things, O'Keeffe discovered the remaining Canyon paintings she had not sent to Stieglitz. It never occurred to her to save these works and, as was her custom, she simply threw them in the trash. She later remembered the windy night in New York when her Canyon paintings, taken out with the garbage, blew all over the street outside the studio.

In this Stieglitz photo, O'Keeffe paints next to a Lake George flower bed. Stieglitz would often ask O'Keeffe to pose for hours at a time.

Working with crude facilities, Stieglitz continued to do some of his best work photographing O'Keeffe. He developed the negatives in the bathroom across the hall and washed them in a basin in the back room. His model was tormented by the ordeal of posing for long hours, barely able to move an eyelash.

When she was not posing for Stieglitz, O'Keeffe focused fully on her own painting. She began using oils again, experimenting with bold, imaginative hues. Regarding her new use of color, O'Keeffe said, "I like the spectacular things."[83] During the fall and winter of 1918–1919, she completed two vibrant abstract series, *Series I* and *Music*, that seemed to capture her new happiness. *Series I* featured plumed, unfurling shapes in roses, blues, and greens. In *Music*, she created a sensual energy with multilayered archways.

Keeping Her Identity

Despite her fierce sense of independence, O'Keeffe allowed Stieglitz to dominate her in many ways. He did not like the smallest changes in their routine or in her appearance. "Stieglitz was always apprehensive about my new things," she recalled.[84] Describing himself to a friend, Stieglitz once wrote, "I'm just a little Impossible at times."[85]

Throughout her long, intense relationship with Stieglitz, Georgia O'Keeffe maintained her own identity. She and Stieglitz respected each other's opinions about art, but she followed her own instincts. For instance, Stieglitz preferred the stark power of O'Keeffe's charcoal drawings and discouraged her use of bright colors. "He had a remarkable color sense, much more subtle than mine," said O'Keeffe. "Mine was obvious and showy in comparison." But following her own intuitive urges, she painted to please herself. "If I stop to think of what others—authorities—would say, I'd not be able to do anything."[86]

During the winter of 1919 O'Keeffe also continued the flower images she had enjoyed many years earlier at Chatham. Using brilliant watercolors, she produced bold and tender studies of scarlet canna lilies. So vibrant were these images, the canna lilies seemed to shout, their colors melting and flowing with a unique sensuality. These early canna lily compositions represented the first series of O'Keeffe's flower subjects, an important body of work in her career.

With the arrival of summer Stieglitz and O'Keeffe returned to Lake George. Oaklawn had been sold: The Stieglitz clan moved to a nearby farm situated on thirty-six acres. The farm featured a white clapboard house that became known as the Hill.

The white clapboard farmhouse that became the Stieglitz family's new summer home in Lake George. Used to being alone, O'Keeffe found the summers with the Stieglitzes oppressive and confining.

O'Keeffe found a small, weathered outbuilding on the property, converting it into a painting studio. She called it the Shanty, and it became her haven for creativity and an escape from the constant swarm of relatives. She walked in the woods, gathering both inspiration and objects to paint before returning to her refuge. Armed with her brushes and a milk glass palette, she spent endless hours working, never allowing visitors nor showing anyone a painting until it was finished.

Needing Time Alone

Arriving back in New York in the fall, O'Keeffe and Stieglitz learned that the building at 291 Fifth Avenue would be demolished. Six months later they learned that the brownstone building where they lived was to be gutted. Once again Lee Stieglitz rescued his brother by inviting the couple to live with him in his home at 60 East 65th Street, near Madison Avenue. O'Keeffe and Stieglitz had several large, comfortable rooms there and continued to dine out each evening.

O'Keeffe had been accustomed to living alone, and at times she found her new life with Stieglitz suffocating. Except for the moves between Lake George and New York, he stubbornly refused to travel. Asserting her independence, O'Keeffe journeyed alone to Maine in the spring of 1920 and had her first view of the Atlantic Ocean. She was glad for the opportunity to be alone, and she cherished the solitude and tranquility of York Beach. Walking on the shore, she marveled at the similarities among the low, flat plane and unbroken horizons of the ocean, the

O'Keeffe as seen through the ever-observant camera lens of Alfred Stieglitz. O'Keeffe became well known as a model after Stieglitz exhibited his photos of her in 1921.

The couple returned to New York in November when O'Keeffe celebrated her thirty-third birthday. She had always wanted a child and realized that time was running out, but Stieglitz did not share her desire to start a family. He wanted O'Keeffe to pursue her career as a painter, and he feared that a child would interfere with her devotion to art. Although she felt a lingering sadness about the decision not to have a family, she also shared Stieglitz's apprehensions. Later she told a writer, "Making a decision to do something and then doing it requires not doing a dozen other things."[87]

Photographs of O'Keeffe Exhibited

plains, and the prairies. She drew inspiration for painting from her new surroundings and gathered strength to face another oppressive summer with the Stieglitz family at Lake George.

In the fall of 1920 Stieglitz and O' Keeffe lingered at the Hill after the hordes of visitors had left, enjoying the tranquility of the Lake George countryside. O'Keeffe completed a series of small domestic still lifes in oil and charcoal using grapes, pears, plums, and apples set in bowls, complemented by a napkin, or alone. She placed the abstract shapes against a flat, undershaded background that highlighted and dramatized the rich, deep colors of the fruit. The plane of the table's edge against the background suggested O'Keeffe's theme of the ocean, the prairie, and the Texas plains against the sky. The creamy texture of the oils demonstrated the continuing influence of her former teacher, William Merritt Chase.

On February 21, 1921, Stieglitz opened an important exhibit, which included his portraits of O'Keeffe, at the Anderson Art Galleries. Excited crowds mobbed the galleries, and much of the public's attention focused on the photographs of O'Keeffe. Although Stieglitz and O'Keeffe had not recognized the dominant theme of artist as model in the portraits, the public found this to be the most interesting angle of the collection. For the first time, people had an opportunity to study an artist, not merely in her work, but through the camera's perspective. Recalling the exhibit, Stieglitz concluded, "This was me at my finest."[88]

Art critic Henry McBride reviewed the show for the *New York Herald:*

There came to notice almost at once . . . some photographs showing every conceivable aspect of O'Keeffe that was a new effort in photography and something new in the way of intro-

Verbal Bouquets from the Critics

Art critic Henry McBride praised O'Keeffe's charcoal drawings in her large solo exhibit, held from January 29 to February 10, 1923, at New York's Anderson Galleries. McBride expressed his recognition of the important role O'Keeffe would play in American art. This excerpt from his review for the New York Herald *appears in* Georgia O'Keeffe: A Life, *by Roxana Robinson.*

"If all those vapors had not been shattered by an electrical bolt from the blue, O'Keeffe would have undoubtedly suffocated from the fumes of self. There would have been no O'Keeffe. In definitely unbosoming her soul she not only finds her own release but advances the cause of art in her country. And the curious and instructive part of the history is that O'Keeffe after venturing with bare feet upon naked sword blades into the land of abstract truth now finds herself a moralist. She is a sort of modern Margaret Fuller sneered at by Nathaniel Hawthorne for a too-great tolerance of sin and finally prayed to by all the super-respectable women of the country for receits [sic] that would keep them from the madhouse. O'Keeffe's next great test probably will be in the same genre. She will be besieged by all her sisters for advice—which will be a supreme danger for her. She is, after all, an artist, and owes more to art than morality. My own advice to her—and I being more moralist than artist can afford advice is, immediately after the show, to get herself to a nunnery."

ducing a budding young artist. . . . It put her at once on the map. Everybody knew the name. She became what is known as a newspaper personality.[89]

As McBride so aptly stated, the exhibit changed O'Keeffe's life in unanticipated ways. Although she had been painting steadily since 1917, the public did not know about her work. Now they saw her primarily as a model. She had become a public figure, sacrificing her private self.

O'Keeffe felt invaded, and she thought the critical jargon silly. In a letter to Mitchell Kennerly, head of the Anderson Galleries, she stated her sentiments toward reviews by art critics:

> The things they write sound so strange and far removed from what I feel about myself. They make me seem like some strange unearthly sort of creature floating in the air breathing in clouds for nourishment. When the truth is that I like beefsteak and like it rare at that.[90]

A year later O'Keeffe had matured as an artist. While she still found artistic reviews distasteful, she accepted them as part of an artist's life. She wrote:

I don't like publicity—it embarrasses me—but as most people buy pictures more through their ears than their eyes—one must be written about and talked about or the people who buy through their ears think your work is no good—and won't buy and one must sell to live—so one must be written about and talked about whether one likes it or not—It always seems they say such stupid things.[91]

In 1923 the first large solo exhibit of O'Keeffe's work opened at the Anderson Galleries, and it was met with a tumult of acclaim. By selling about twenty paintings, she generated her first income since leaving the West Texas Normal School in Canyon. The artist's words in the exhibit's catalog reflected her new level of comfort in expressing herself.

I say that I do not want to have this exhibition because, among other reasons, there are so many exhibitions that it seems ridiculous for me to add to the mess, but I guess I'm lying. I probably do want to see my things hang on a wall as other things hang so as to be able to place them in my mind in relation to other things I have seen done. And I presume, if I must be honest, that I am also interested in what anybody else has to say about them and also in what they don't say because that means something to me too.[92]

The 1923 exhibit was followed by another show the following year. O'Keeffe wrote, "I may have another exhibition this year—Am not sure yet—don't much care—but I've done well enough to be talked about and written about more and more."[93]

When Stieglitz finally received a divorce in September 1924, he pressed O'Keeffe to marry him. Although she felt no need to be legally married, she gave in to Stieglitz's wishes. They were married in Cliffside Park, New Jersey, on December 11, 1924. However, O'Keeffe felt strongly about the issue of retaining her own name and always bristled when called Mrs. Stieglitz. Later she told a writer, "I've had a hard time hanging on to my name, but I hang on to it with my teeth. I like getting what I've got on my own."[94]

The couple continued their pattern of life divided between winters in New York City and summers at the Hill. In 1925 they moved into the thirty-fourth floor of the Shelton Hotel, in one of New York's newest skyscrapers. Demonstrating her diversity as an artist during this time, Georgia painted twenty skyscraper compositions, including *New York with Moon* (1925) and *City Night* (1926).

The Flower Series

While O'Keeffe painted monumental skyscrapers, she was also painting an exquisite series of flowers. A few years earlier in Lake George, she had passed a florist shop that displayed calla lilies in the window. Struck by the majesty of the regal white blossoms, she began to paint a series featuring the lilies on rectangular panels. Later, O'Keeffe described her inspiration for the great flowers:

That was in the 20s, and everything was going so fast. Nobody had time to reflect. . . . There was a cup and saucer, a spoon and a flower. Well, the

O'Keeffe abandoned her usual rural themes to paint more than twenty skyscraper compositions, including New York with Moon *(1925).*

flowers never before observed. O'Keeffe reasoned that if an artist could depict mountains as small in a composition, then certainly a flower could be made immense.

During this period O'Keeffe demonstrated her diversity as an artist, continuing to expand the calla lily series she had begun in 1922. The flower studies proved to be one of her greatest artistic contributions. The calla lily panels first appeared in Stieglitz's *Seven Americans* exhibit at the Anderson Galleries in 1925, the year Anderson opened the Intimate Gallery, known simply as the Room. Sharing the show with six male artists, Georgia received recognition for her collection. "America seems to have produced a woman painter comparable to the best women poets and novelists," wrote one critic.[96]

When another O'Keeffe exhibit opened at the Room on February 27, 1928, a French collector, who has remained anonymous to this day, inquired about the price of the flower series. Stieglitz did not know how to respond. To test the Frenchman's reaction, he made up a ridiculously high price, $25,000. Without hesitation the collector agreed to buy the six panels for Stieglitz's asking price. It was the highest price ever brought by O'Keeffe, by a woman artist, or by a living American artist.

O'Keeffe Gains Fame

The sale of the calla lily series made O'Keeffe famous, and Stieglitz resented the attention his wife received. He had always been a difficult person, but now his dark, brooding moods intensified, placing severe strains on their relationship.

flower was perfectly beautiful. It was exquisite, but it was so small you really could not appreciate it for yourself. So then and there I decided to paint that flower in all its beauty. If I could paint that flower in a huge scale, then you could not ignore its beauty.[95]

A celebration of color and texture, the calla lily paintings suggested a new approach to painting. Because each flower is huge, the compositions demand attention. The viewer notes exquisite details about the

Flower Paintings

During her long career O'Keeffe painted more than two hundred flower paintings. In One Hundred Flowers, *editor Nicholas Calloway discusses these compositions.*

"Georgia O'Keeffe was not a flower painter. She may be, however, the greatest painter of flowers in the history of Western Art. She always stressed the primacy of the artist's vision over subject matter, and staunchly resisted those who would categorize her works by genre, school or gender.

It would be incorrect to assess O'Keeffe's contribution to twentieth century American art on the basis of the flower paintings alone. In her exhibitions and books, she took care to ensure that all of her themes—abstractions, desert landscapes, city views, bones, shells, flowers and other natural forms—be seen in relation to each other. . . .

By the end of her 98 years she made over 200 flower paintings, the majority . . . from 1912 to 1932.

The first large-scale canvasses were completed in 1924 . . . and were shown in 1925 at the 'Seven Americans' exhibition held by Stieglitz at the Anderson Galleries.

When these giant flowers were exhibited, they caused a sensation, eliciting a host of reactions ranging from critical raves to outrage to awe. One reviewer said that confronting an O'Keeffe painting tends to make the viewer feel 'as if we humans were butterflies.' Even Stieglitz's first reaction to them was equivocal; when O'Keeffe called him into her studio to show him 'Petunia No. 2' (1924), his first response was, 'Well, Georgia, I don't know how you're going to get away with anything like that—you aren't planning to show it, are you?'"

The White Flower *is typical of O'Keeffe's flower paintings in that it reveals a tremendous amount of detail.*

O'Keeffe's stunning flower series suggested a new approach to painting. Pictured is Two Calla Lilies on Pink *(1928).*

During the summer of 1928 Stieglitz suffered a heart attack. O'Keeffe devoted much of the following year to caring for him, painting very little. What she completed was uncharacteristically dull. When her works were exhibited at the Anderson Galleries in 1929, the critics were polite but cool in their reviews.

At the age of forty-one O'Keeffe realized that she was drifting. She was unaccustomed to taking care of another person. Her life with Stieglitz was dictated by his likes and preferences. She felt trapped, uninspired, and creatively stymied. Thus she was pleased when a friend, the painter Dorothy Brett, issued an invitation to visit her in Taos, New Mexico. Brett understood that O'Keeffe needed rest and the stimulation of a new environment. Rebecca Strand, Paul Strand's wife, offered to make the trip to Taos, too.

The idea of going to New Mexico deeply appealed to O'Keeffe, who remembered her visit there years earlier with her sister Claudia. She had always been haunted by the stark beauty of the Southwest and the light that so clearly illuminated the forms on the desert. She knew Taos had become a colony of artists, boasting such well-known figures as author D. H. Lawrence.

Stieglitz strongly opposed the idea of being left alone for the summer, but O'Keeffe realized that the trip was a matter of self-preservation. As an artist, she recognized the importance of renewing artistic inspiration. As a woman living with a demanding individual, she longed for solitude. "I have to keep some of myself or I wouldn't have anything left to give," she told a friend. "Giving is difficult—almost to[o] difficult."[97]

Chapter

7 Transitions

As Georgia O'Keeffe and Rebecca "Beck" Strand traveled to New Mexico by train in the summer of 1929, the artist's mood brightened with each westward mile. The two women arrived in Santa Fe and immediately took in the local entertainment by attending a traditional corn dance. There they met Mabel Dodge, the wealthy art patron, and her companion Tony Luhan.

Dodge insisted that the easterners stay at her ranch near Taos, and O'Keeffe was housed in a studio there, situated in a round building constructed from adobe brick. The studio's large windows provided an excellent view of the dark Taos mountain and the bright meadow surrounding the little house. O'Keeffe was mesmerized by New Mexico's beauty and landscapes, featuring everything from hot springs to snow-covered peaks. In a letter to Paul Strand, she wrote:

> Taos is a high, wide, sage-covered plain. In the evening, with the sun at your back, it looks like an ocean, like water. The color up there is different . . . the blue-green of the sage and the mountains, the wildflowers in bloom. It's a different kind of color from any I'd ever seen—there's nothing like that in north Texas or even in Colorado. And it's not just the color that attracted me, either. The world is so wide up there, so big.[98]

O'Keeffe and friend Rebecca Strand during one of their trips to New Mexico.

In a gesture symbolic of her desire for independence and mobility, O'Keeffe bought a black model A Ford and learned to drive. With Tony Luhan and Beck Strand bravely offering driving lessons, she proved to be somewhat reckless behind the wheel. "The bridges here are only wide enough for angels to fly over," she wrote a friend, "so they give me great difficulty."[99]

As O'Keeffe had hoped, the magnificent landscape renewed her creative energies. Everything she saw sparked new ideas for painting. Driving around Abiquiu, west of Taos, she was intrigued by crosses that seemed to rise mysteriously out of the desert. The local people claimed that they had been erected by Penitentes, a secret religious society dating back to medieval Spain. The painting *Black Cross, New Mexico* is one of O'Keeffe's most powerful works.

O'Keeffe also painted a mission church at Ranchos des Taos but instead of including the entire structure in her composi-

O'Keeffe found the landscapes of New Mexico infinitely inspiring. Her painting Black Cross, New Mexico *(1929) was inspired by the mysterious crosses that she found planted in isolated locations.*

Inspiration to Other Artists

C. Kay Scott, an aspiring painter, expressed her feelings about the importance of O'Keeffe's work in a letter to O'Keeffe that was printed in an exhibition catalogue in 1928.

"My heart finds in your pictures a deep satisfaction . . . this comes from . . . a fearless clarity of vision . . . perfect purity of purpose. . . . This amazing psychic balance comes from a courageous self-acceptance, without which no real and lasting art is possible. With this to stand on, you have dared, and loved, to paint what seems to me the organs of the spiritual universe . . . you do what is your own, and I believe that your own is significant to painting and to our time."

tion, she painted only segments of the church, affirming her belief that in a painting, segments often make a stronger statement than a complete picture. One night, as O'Keeffe was lying on a bench, she was struck by the image of the stars and sky through the branches of a pine tree. The painting that resulted, *The Lawrence Tree*, remained one of her favorite compositions.

Returning to New York

O'Keeffe returned to her sixty-five-year-old husband in August to find him in good health. Although Stieglitz had missed her, he saw the evidence that the trip had had positive effects. O'Keeffe resumed her work with vigor, completing some paintings she had begun in New Mexico while beginning new works.

In October 1929 the Great Depression thrust the country into a deep economic chasm of increasing unemployment and poverty. Stieglitz remained calm in the face of the country's mounting gloom. He opened a new gallery, An American Place, at 509 Madison Avenue.

An American Place's first show in February 1930 featured O'Keeffe's most recent New Mexico works. The exhibit ignited much controversy. Some critics saw O'Keeffe's compositions as strange, describing her crosses as hysterical, while others liked the New Mexican influences on the artist's creative endeavors. Critic Henry McBride wrote, "It is intellectually thrilling to find Miss O'Keeffe adopting so quickly the Spanish idea that where life manifests itself in great ebullience there too is death most formidable."[100]

A shift in the political climate was felt throughout the country that winter. Elements of unrest sparked by the Depression combined forces with a movement of long standing in favor of representational art to produce a new view of the role of the arts in American society. Increasingly, many artists believed it was their mission to speak out against social injustice.

In March 1930 O'Keeffe accepted an invitation to debate Michael Gold, the zealous editor of the liberal publication *New Masses*, about the social issues surrounding artistic expression. Debating was an unusual departure for the private O'Keeffe, but she proved to be a formidable

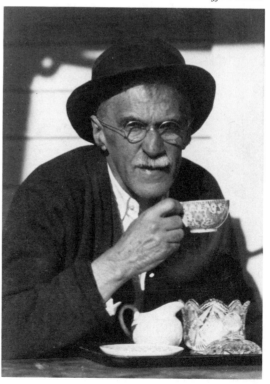

O'Keeffe returned from New Mexico to her always difficult husband (pictured) in August 1929. During the Depression, Stieglitz opened a new gallery called An American Place to exhibit O'Keeffe's work.

The Crosses

When O'Keeffe visited New Mexico in 1929, she was impressed by the crosses erupting from the desert, said to be constructed by a religious group, the Penitentes. A series of compositions featuring these crosses was exhibited at Stieglitz's gallery. Art critic Henry McBride wrote about the series for a newspaper in 1930. This excerpt is taken from Georgia O'Keeffe: An Exhibition, *edited by Mitchell A. Wilder.*

"'Any one who doesn't feel the crosses,' said Miss O'Keeffe, whom I fortunately encountered at the private view, 'simply doesn't get that country.' . . . So much is brought back to us of the frivolities of the tourist colony at Taos, so much is said of the added pulse-beats that are caused by the high-powered ozones of that locality, that it is intellectually thrilling to find Miss O'Keeffe adopting so quickly the Spanish idea that where life manifests itself in greatest ebullience there too is death most formidable.

The 'Crosses' run through several sets of chromatics and emotions. There is 'St. Francis of Assisi' in pale blues and turquoise, for those who have given over the world completely and live or attempt to live on the spiritual heights. There are several crosses for those who have dabbled slightly both in sin and virtue and are not yet certain which way they are going; and finally there is the great 'Parsifal' cross posed blackly and ponderously against sky of molten crimsons and vermillions, and with purple velvet mountains in the distance. The mind pauses in contemplation of this picture. In fact, it is distinctly not for the mind but for the 'subconscious.' A gallery is no place for it. It ought to be viewed in church."

opponent. O'Keeffe took the position that art should not have to right social injustice, or even represent it.

O'Keeffe had always been interested in women's rights. As she told a writer, "All the male artists I knew, of course, made it very plain that as a woman I couldn't hope to make it—I might as well stop painting."[101] However, by resisting male dictates in art and through use of her artistic intuition, she had shown that a woman could succeed. O'Keeffe maintained that her compositions did not have to reflect political positions. She felt that her paintings did not need to literally represent political schemes such as the oppression of women. As she told a writer for *New York World:*

The subject matter of a painting should never obscure its form and color, which are real thematic contents. . . . So I have no difficulty in contending that my paintings of a flower may be just as much a product of this age as a cartoon about the freedom of women—or the working class—or anything else.[102]

Emotional and defensive, Gold passionately argued the opposite point of view, that the first obligation of art should be the literal representation of societal problems. However, when O'Keeffe asked him if he felt women were oppressed as a group, he snapped, "I'm afraid it doesn't seem very important to me if the pampered bourgeoise in her rose-colored boudoir gets equal rights or not."[103]

O'Keeffe calmly countered his argument by citing examples from her own life. She concluded her remarks by stating, "You may be seeking the freedom of humanity, but you want to make art a tool—and the worst of it is that you must cheapen art to appeal to any mass, and your mass artists will inevitably become bad artists."[104]

Emotional Distress

O'Keeffe returned to New Mexico in the summer of 1930, over Stieglitz's continued objections. During her absences he suffered from depression and other ailments, but his loneliness was eased that summer by the company of a younger woman, Dorothy Norman. A writer and art enthusiast, Norman began to spend a great deal of time with Stieglitz. She helped him with tasks at the studio such as fund-raising and bookkeeping. Stieglitz was enchanted by Norman and he began to photograph her as he had once photographed O'Keeffe, posing her in similar poses dressed in black.

That summer O'Keeffe painted *Near Abiquiu*, showing the tranquility of the curved hills, interrupted by an occasional sharp peak. "It was the shapes of the hills there that fascinated me," she said. "The reddish sand hills with the dark mesas behind them. It seemed as though no matter how far you walked you could never get

Near Abiquiu *(1930) depicts the curved hills of New Mexico that so fascinated O'Keeffe.*

into those dark hills, although I walked great distances."[105]

When O'Keeffe returned from New Mexico and learned of her husband's relationship with the younger woman, she was devastated. Emotionally distraught, she could not paint during the winter of 1930–31, and returned to New Mexico for two months during the summer of 1932. During her visit, she painted the hauntingly beautiful *Desert Abstraction*, featuring the horizon of desert and sky. She also walked on the desert and was struck by the dry, bleached animal bones lying there, recalling her attraction to the remains she had found in Texas. She gathered some of the bones and had them sent to Lake George. Describing her affinity for the bones, she wrote:

> To me they are as beautiful as anything I know. To me they are strangely more living than the animals walking around. . . . The bones seem to cut sharply to the center of something that is keenly alive on the desert even tho' it is vast and empty and untouchable—and knows no kindness with all its beauty.[106]

The Skull Paintings

Returning to the Hill that summer, O'Keeffe unpacked a skull she had found on the desert and sat it on the dining room table where a guest had laid a pair of blue pajamas. She had been working with some cloth flowers, and she impulsively placed one in the skull's eye. She liked the colors combined with the interesting shapes and textures of the bones and was inspired to paint *Cow's Skull—Red,*

White, and Blue. Recalling her enthusiasm for the painting, she later commented:

> I was quite excited over our country and I knew almost any one of those great minds (intellectuals and artists in the East) would have been living in Europe if it had been possible for them. They didn't even want to live in New York—how was the Great American Thing going to happen? So as I painted along on my cow's skull on blue, I thought to myself, "I'll make an American painting. They will not think it great with the red stripes down the sides—Red, White, and Blue, but they will notice it."[107]

When O'Keeffe's bone paintings were exhibited in December 1931, they drew mixed reactions. "A splendid salutation of

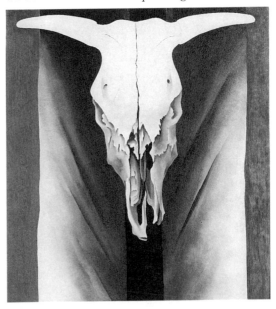

Cow's Skull—Red, White, and Blue *(1931) was O'Keeffe's first painting featuring a skull—a theme that would become one of her favorites. Commenting on her choice of colors, O'Keeffe claimed that she wanted to do an American painting.*

The Colors and Flowers of Her Palette

No artist used color with the same intensity and imagination as O'Keeffe. Here, Nicholas Calloway discusses O'Keeffe's combination of colors and flowers in One Hundred Flowers.

"O'Keeffe's palette was as startling as the gigantic scale of her canvases. No American painter had explored such radical combinations of color nor such an astonishing intensity of hue. The colors favored at that time by her contemporaries and colleagues were for the most part 'dreary' as she called them—somber and low-toned. The flower paintings are as much about pure color—sometimes riotous, sometimes almost purely monochromatic—as they are about subject matter. In the 1950s, O'Keeffe wrote about the 'White Flower' (1929).

'Whether the flower or the color is the focus I do not know. I do know that the flower is painted large to convey to you my experience of the flower—if it is not color.'

Her friend, the painter Charles Demuth, described O'Keeffe's color sense in the brochure accompanying her 1927 exhibit at the Intimate Gallery: 'Flowers and flames. And colour. Colour as colour, not as volume, or light—only as colour. The last mad throb of red, just as it turns green, the ultimate shriek of orange calling upon all the blues of heaven for relief or for support; these Georgia O'Keeffe is able to use. In her canvases each colour almost regains the fun it must have felt within itself, on forming the first rainbow.'"

the dead," proclaimed one critic who interpreted the paintings as a metaphor for death; but others understood O'Keeffe's attractions to the skulls.[108] Henry McBride wrote:

Looking at these original works purely from the painting angle they are of Miss O'Keeffe's best, and for my part I imagine that she saw these ghostly relics merely as elegant shapes charged with solemn mystery. Like the plant forms and shells . . . that she so inordinately [excessively] admires, these bones to her are part of nature's marvelous handiwork, to be taken at face value and reverenced for their intrinsic form.[109]

O'Keeffe decided to remain at Lake George during the summer of 1932. In August she traveled with an artist friend, visiting Canada for the first time. There, they drove through the lush farmland

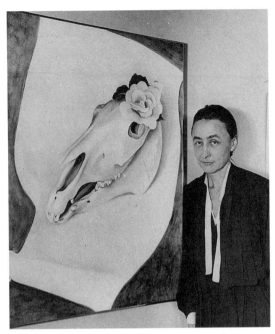

O'Keeffe stands in front of Life and Death, *another of her skull paintings. Many critics found the skulls morbid, but others found the clean lines and bleached coloring fascinating, as O'Keeffe herself did.*

along the St. Lawrence River, painting throughout their journey. During their trek Georgia was intrigued by the local barns and painted a series of these structures, including *White Canadian Barn II.*

Illness

O'Keeffe had entered and won a competition sponsored by New York's Museum of Modern Art. Her design, *Manhattan,* would be featured on a large mural in the women's lounge at the Radio City Music Hall scheduled to open in December 1932.

Stieglitz strongly opposed O'Keeffe's plans. He disliked murals and felt the $1,500 fee O'Keeffe would receive was inadequate. Without O'Keeffe's knowledge, Stieglitz talked to the director of the project, Donald Deskey, encouraging him not to have the job done by his wife, whom he characterized as a child, not responsible for her actions. Deskey rejected Stieglitz's pleas. O'Keeffe would paint her design.

During the fall O'Keeffe became increasingly troubled. The mural proved to be a difficult project. She had never attempted painting on such a massive scale, and the work fell behind schedule. Her frustrations about the mural combined with her concerns over her husband's continuing relationship with the younger woman, Dorothy Norman. O'Keeffe was on the verge of emotional exhaustion.

Radio City Music Hall was to open two days after Christmas, but the canvas for the mural was not mounted until November. When O'Keeffe inspected the work, she discovered that a section of canvas had not been installed according to her directions. The seemingly minor problem proved to be the straw that broke the camel's back, and she fled the building in tears. The next day, Stieglitz informed Deskey that O'Keeffe was suffering from nervous exhaustion and would not be able to complete the mural.

O'Keeffe rested at Lake George, but her condition worsened. She suffered severe headaches, insomnia, loss of appetite, and difficulty in breathing. On February 1, 1933, she was admitted to Doctor's Hospital in Manhattan. The diagnosis was psychoneurosis (a nervous breakdown).

Chapter 8 New Mexico

O'Keeffe faced months of complete rest following her release from the hospital on March 25, 1933. A friend, Marjorie Content, accompanied her to Bermuda, where she wrote to Beck Strand that she was enjoying the ocean and the sun: "It is warm and slow and the sea such a lovely clear greenish blue. I have done little but sit— However, the sitting is good."[110]

Following her hospitalization, O'Keeffe realized that she must make changes in her life. Her husband's relationship with Dorothy Norman had been a primary reason for her emotional collapse.

Alfred Stieglitz, who had been largely responsible for launching O'Keeffe's successful career as an artist, was a demanding, selfish individual. O'Keeffe once confessed to a friend that she felt Stieglitz was happiest when she was sick in bed. Then he knew exactly where she was and what she was doing. He refused to travel with his wife to the places she enjoyed, but he resented her traveling alone. Instead of seeing her trips as a vital source of artistic inspiration, he pouted and made O'Keeffe feel guilty for leaving him.

Finally, however, O'Keeffe learned the importance of meeting her own needs. The nervous breakdown had been a difficult experience, but she reached a valuable conclusion. She wrote to a friend, "I

Selfish and demanding, Stieglitz wanted O'Keeffe within his sight at all times, a tendency that did not go well with O'Keeffe's need for independence.

am divided between my man and a life with him—and something of the outdoors that is in my blood—and that I know I will never get rid of—I have to get along with my divided self the best way I can."[111]

O'Keeffe did not paint for several years after returning from Bermuda. She realized that she had been to the edge of a dangerous abyss and that regaining her emotional and physical energies would

Following O'Keeffe's nervous breakdown, an aging Stieglitz (left) attempted to be more sympathetic to her needs. Even though the relationship was troubled from the start, the two remained together.

require time. She renewed her friendship with a young black author, Jean Toomer, who she felt was sensitive to her feelings during those difficult months. She wrote him a moving letter, comparing her soul to the American soil where she had taken root as a child:

> My center does not come from my mind—it feels in me like a plot of warm moist well tilled earth with the sun shining hot on it. . . . It seems I would rather feel starkly empty than let anything be planted that cannot be tended to the fullest possibility of its growth . . . my plot of earth must be tended with absurd care. . . . By myself first—and if second by someone else, it must be with absolute trust. . . . It seems it would be very difficult for me to live if it were wrecked again just now.[112]

Following his wife's illness, Stieglitz learned to be more sensitive to O'Keeffe's needs. He conceded that her trips to New Mexico were vital, and he encouraged her to seek new inspiration. O'Keeffe returned to Lake George in the summer of 1933, but she remained weak and forlorn. She described her condition in a letter to Beck Strand:

> I just sit in my effortless soup and wait for myself. I do not mean that I make no effort to do things that seem difficult. It seems I never made such efforts to do things in all my life put together—it is that all the little daily doings are such an effort—And the worst of my fatigue is a suffering in my nerves that is much worse than physical pain— I don't really get tired physically.[113]

In February 1934 Stieglitz held a retrospective of O'Keeffe's works at An American Place, featuring the paintings she had done from 1915 to 1927. The Metropolitan Museum of Art in New York purchased *Black Flower and Blue Larkspur*, one of her earlier New Mexico works shown at the exhibit. The museum's purchase signaled O'Keeffe's acceptance as a respected artist and gave her financial security.

Discovering Ghost Ranch

O'Keeffe returned to New Mexico in June, apprehensive about leaving Stieglitz alone, but filled with a strong resolve to live her own life. As she drove through the state in her model A, she searched for a mysterious place known as Ghost Ranch. She had heard about the ranch during earlier visits but had been unable to locate it. One day, while visiting the town of Alcalde, south of Taos and Abiquiu, she noticed a vehicle with "GR" painted on the side. Upon inquiring, she learned that the letters stood for Ghost Ranch. The driver of the vehicle gave O'Keeffe directions and with a sense of adventure, she set out to find the ranch.

After driving through forty miles of beautiful desert terrain, O'Keeffe spotted an animal skull marking the Ghost Ranch turnoff. She was filled with the same feelings she had experienced during her first train trip west to New Mexico, when an inner voice had told her this was her land. This was a part of New Mexico that she had never seen, and the land appealed to something deep in her soul.

O'Keeffe continued driving until she found Ghost Ranch, a group of ranch houses built around a golden mesa.

Black Flower and Blue Larkspur *(1934) was purchased by the Metropolitan Museum of Art in New York. The purchase signaled a widespread acceptance of O'Keeffe's work.*

O'Keeffe poses coquettishly with Orville Cox, head wrangler at Ghost Ranch.

Owned by Arthur Newton Pack, publisher of *Nature* magazine, the dude ranch catered to wealthy guests who desired to experience the Wild West while staying in luxurious accommodations. The idea of being a guest at a dude ranch held no appeal for O'Keeffe, but she found the scenery more beautiful than anything she had ever seen. Although she planned to stay only one night, she found an empty cottage on the grounds and remained until her return to Lake George in the fall. For the next decade, O'Keeffe would return annually to this part of New Mexico.

Located on the eastern edge of the Jemez mountain range, Ghost Ranch was situated in what geologists call the Abiquiu Quadrangle. O'Keeffe biographer Roxana Robinson described the landscape.

> There are a few places as spectacular on the Northern continent, but not many. Geologically it is rather complicated; visually it is breathtaking. The high, flat bottomland is broken irregularly by vast cliffs and low hills in

The Bones and the Blue

In the New York Sun *on January 15, 1944, art critic Henry McBride wrote about O'Keeffe's series of paintings* The Bones and the Blue. *This is an excerpt from his article entitled "Miss O'Keeffe's Bones: An Artist of the Western Plains Just Misses Abstract."*

"[Georgia O'Keeffe] has written a piece for her current exhibition explaining why she makes pictures from the bleached bones of the desert—and it is very good. It is practically a poem. But anyway it is very good.

'I have picked flowers where I found them—

'Have picked up sea shells and rocks and pieces of wood where there were sea shells and rocks and pieces of wood that I liked.

'When I found the beautiful white bones on the desert I picked them up and took them home too

'I have used these things to say what is to me the wideness and wonder of the world as I live in it

'A pelvis bone has always been useful to any animal that has it—quite as useful as a head I suppose. For years in the country the pelvis lay about the house indoors and out—always underfoot—seen and not seen as such things can be—seen in many different ways. I do not remember picking up the first one but I remember from when I first noticed them always knowing I would one day be painting them. A particularly beautiful one that I found on the mountain where I went fishing this summer started me working on them

'I was the sort of child that ate around the raisin on the cookie and ate around the hole of the doughnut saving either the raisins or the hole for the last and best.

'So probably—not having changed much—when I started painting the pelvis bones I was most interested in the holes in the bones—what I saw through them—particularly in the blue form holding them up in the sun against the sky as one is apt to do when one seems to have more sky than earth in one's world—

'They were most wonderful against the Blue—that Blue that will always be there as it is now after all man's destruction is finished

'I have tried to paint the Bones and the Blue.' "

astonishing colors. The rock forma-tions are Mesozoic—roughly between one and two hundred million years old. The cliffs and hills stand like a ge-ological model, each layer a demon-stration of earthly possibility.[114]

In this magnificent setting, O'Keeffe picked up her brushes once again, paint-ing with a renewed passion. The clear air made it possible for her to see for miles, creating an illusion that the majestic pink cliffs were deceptively close. She painted the haunting hills in shades altered by the sun and the clouds. At times, the gentle curves were pink and orange, at other times red and purple. She remembered seeing those hills: "From where I stood it seemed I could see all over the world . . . and I like the feel of the wind against me when I get up high."[115]

O'Keeffe also painted and collected the desert's natural artifacts—stones,

branches, and bones. Each morning she set out in her model A to explore some new aspect of the land. She worked all day in the intense heat, painting from 7:00 A.M. until after 5:00 P.M., occasionally resting in the only available shade beneath her car.

Just as O'Keeffe had enjoyed playing alone with her dollhouse as a child, she still preferred the solitude for working. Her friend Dorothy Brett observed, "When you got to know Georgia, she was a very, very nice person. But she had a rather cold front that made things a little difficult for her and for everybody else. It's a horrid thing to say, but I think she was bored with people."[116]

O'Keeffe increased the length of her visits to Ghost Ranch in 1935 and 1936. During these years, she completed some of the most important work of her career. Her love for the New Mexico landscape was reflected in *Blue River* (1935) and *Red Hills and Pedernal* (1936). In *Ram's Head—*

Ram's Head—White Hollyhock *(1935) was painted while at Ghost Ranch, New Mexico. In the terrain of New Mexico, O'Keeffe finally discovered what she called "her land."*

White Hollyhock (1935) O'Keeffe floated a skull and a delicate flower against a gray sky with the orange, tree-dotted hills below. Lewis Mumford of the *New Yorker* wrote, "Not only is it a piece of consummate craftsmanship, but it likewise possesses that mysterious force, that hold upon the hidden soul, which distinguishes important communication from the casual reports of the eye."[117]

As O'Keeffe's artistic career blossomed, money was no longer a worry for her and Stieglitz. In 1936 the couple moved into a posh penthouse apartment at 405 East 54th Street.

Rancho de los Burros

In 1937 O'Keeffe arrived at Ghost Ranch to learn that no cabin was available for her. Arthur Pack set her up in a simple adobe house, Rancho de los Burros, a few miles from Ghost Ranch. "As soon as I saw it, I knew I must have it," she later recalled. "I can't understand people who want something badly but don't grab for it. I grabbed."[118] Although it would be three more years before she actually purchased the property from Pack, O'Keeffe considered Rancho de los Burros her own from her first summer there. That summer she met the photographer Ansel Adams, who later became famous for his black-and-white photographs of the region. Adams shared O'Keeffe's love of the Southwest.

The seclusion of Rancho de los Burros appealed to O'Keeffe's need for solitude, and the house commanded a magnificent view of the cliffs she loved. She frequently painted the Pedernal, a flat-topped mesa about ten miles away. "It's my private

mountain. It belongs to me," she later joked. "God told me if I painted it enough, I could have it."[119] She also painted the adobe structure she had come to love, *The House I Live In*, in 1937.

During those years following the Great Depression, American art was undergoing a period of redefinition, searching for pure American art forms. O'Keeffe never concerned herself with such trends, but she later described the era:

> There was a lot of talk in New York then—during the late twenties and early thirties—about the Great American Painting. It was like the Great American Novel. People wanted to "do" the American scene. I had gone back and forth across the country several times by then and some of the current ideas about the American scene struck me as pretty ridiculous. To them, the American scene was a dilapitated house with a broken down buckboard out front and a horse that looked like a skeleton. I knew America was very rich, very lush. . . . For goodness sake, I thought, the people who talk about the American scene don't know anything about it.[120]

Ironically, by not conforming to anyone else's dictates about American art, O'Keeffe was indeed becoming the consummate American artist. There was nothing regional about her work—she painted objects and scenes from every part of the country, celebrating nature in all her forms, from the smallest flower to regal mountain ranges. Critic Mumford wrote, "No matter what Miss O'Keeffe's further development, one can already say pretty confidently, I think, that she will occupy a place in painting similar to that which

The Barn Paintings

Throughout her life, O'Keeffe's artistic eye remained deeply rooted in her rural Wisconsin heritage. In 1932 she traveled to Canada's Gaspé region, where she was inspired to paint a series of barn compositions, the most well known being White Canadian Barn II. *These paintings were exhibited at An American Place in 1933. Art critic Henry McBride reviewed her work for the* New York Sun *in January 1933.*

"Star of An American Place Shines in Undiminished Luster

In my own case, I find I am more mystified and impressed, this year, by the series of pictures of barns than by anything else. They are very elegant. Of course, the exquisite precision with which these barns are placed upon canvas is understandable, being intellectually arrived at, but the solidity of these edifices patiently built of tenderly pure pigment is something I do not understand. The little one in the corner gallery has all the force of statement of a Picasso, yet in Picasso you can see the artist applying power, while in the O'Keeffe barn the artist seems to stand aside and let the barn do it all by itself. That's why I say the best O'Keeffes seem wished upon the canvas—the mechanics have been so beautifully concealed.

Hardby [Nearby], this barn in the little corner gallery is one of Miss O'Keeffe's obvious manifestations of occultism. It is a rendition of a tall and slender cross by the seashore, a monument to some New England seafaring person. It is as bleak as a play by Eugene O'Neill with settings by Robert Edmond Jones, and it gets you as surely as their work does."

Emily Dickinson has in poetry. The little Amherst witch knew what she was about; and so does O'Keeffe."[121]

Becoming America's Artist

As her reputation grew, O'Keeffe's work was commissioned by large commercial concerns. In 1936 she completed a massive painting featuring white jimson blossoms for Elizabeth Arden, the cosmetics magnate. Arden paid $10,000 for the composition, which was displayed in her Manhattan exercise salon. The Steuben Glass Company commissioned O'Keeffe to create a delicate lily design, which they engraved on crystal bowls that sold for $500 each.

In 1938 the Dole Pineapple Company flew O'Keeffe to Hawaii, on commission, to use her art on their products and for

Jimson Weed (1936), the painting O'Keeffe did for Elizabeth Arden, was displayed in Arden's Manhattan exercise salon.

male school at the time. In 1939 she was chosen as one of twelve most outstanding women of the past fifty years by the New York World's Fair Tomorrow Committee; one of her paintings, *Sunset, Long Island*, was chosen to represent New York State at the fair.

O'Keeffe had been traveling and working feverishly since 1934. In 1939 she began to exhibit some of the same symptoms that had preceded her illness in 1933: exhaustion, headaches, insomnia, and loss of appetite. Her doctor ordered complete rest, and she remained in New York during the summer of 1939. Fortunately, she quickly regained her strength and easily recovered.

advertising. She asked to stay with the field workers so she could be near the pineapple fields, but Dole officials felt it was silly for a famous artist to stay in such surroundings. When O'Keeffe later submitted two designs, one of a red ginger flower, the other of a papaya tree, Dole Company executives expressed disappointment that neither design was the pineapple bud. The art director of N. W. Ayers, Dole's advertising agency, had a pineapple bud flown to O'Keeffe in New York and she produced a painting of the plant, which the company used in promotional pieces.

Increasingly, Georgia O'Keeffe was recognized as the important American artist she had become. In 1938 *Life* magazine featured a photo essay on the painter and her work. That same year, the College of William and Mary in Williamsburg, Virginia, awarded her an honorary doctor of fine arts degree. Ironically, she had not been able to attend the college when she lived in Williamsburg, since it was an all-

Putting Down Roots

In 1940 O'Keeffe purchased Rancho de los Burros and eight acres from Arthur Pack.

Stieglitz lectures on O'Keeffe's work at an exhibition. He is talking about O'Keeffe's painting The Bone.

She considered it the best investment she ever made, and it marked the beginning of one of the most productive periods of her artistic life. Immediately she began making changes, enlarging windows and knocking out a wall to create a studio.

Because the ranch was so isolated, she had to drive eighty miles just to purchase food. The desert climate was not suitable for a vegetable garden, and she existed largely on canned foods. Rattlesnakes regularly crawled into the adobe dwelling, seeking warmth from the fireplace, and she routinely scooped them up with a shovel and deposited them outside, on the desert sand.

Eventually she hired a housekeeper, Maria Cabot. With Cabot's assistance, O'Keeffe no longer concerned herself with domestic responsibilities. She was free to paint ten or twelve hours daily. Sometimes the two women set out on camping trips, exploring the hills on horseback.

World War II

While O'Keeffe painted in the isolated environment of America's Southwest, the world stood on the brink of war. As Hitler's armies marched through Europe, many Americans hoped that the United States would be able to stay out of the conflict. On December 7, 1941, however, the Japanese bombed America's naval base in Pearl Harbor, Hawaii, and the United States declared war on Japan the following day.

By 1942 FBI agents began snooping around the ranch. Not much later, Arthur Pack received security clearance, and soon mysterious visitors were taking their rest at his ranch on weekends. Pack was told that

O'Keeffe with prominent art collector Mrs. Chester Dale. As O'Keeffe's work gained in popularity, her works were more sought after and increased in value.

no questions were to be asked of these men, but soon their mission was clear. They were working at the Los Alamos National Laboratory, twenty miles from Ranchos de los Burros. There, researchers developed the elaborate weaponry needed to detonate an atomic explosion.

In the spring of 1942 O'Keeffe was reunited with her beloved Aunt Ollie when she traveled to Wisconsin to accept an honorary doctor of letters degree from the University of Wisconsin in Madison. Also receiving this honor was General Douglas MacArthur, commander of U.S. forces in the Pacific. It pleased O'Keeffe that the university had selected both an artist and a general in time of war.

During that year O'Keeffe was approached by Daniel Catton Rich, curator of painting at the Art Institute of Chicago, who wanted to hold a major retrospective of O'Keeffe's works. The artist, who arrived in Chicago in January 1943 to oversee the staging of the exhibition, demanded that the violet gallery walls be

O'Keeffe in 1943, the year that the Art Institute of Chicago staged a major retrospective of her work.

traveling difficult, and she carefully planned her trips, using horseback more frequently at the ranch for desert treks. From 1943 to 1945, she painted a new series, focused on pelvic bones she had found on the New Mexico desert. At first she juxtaposed the bones against the planes of sky and landscape, but as the series progressed, she became intrigued with the possibilities provided by the natural openings of the bone. She used bone, opening, and sky to focus the viewer's attention solely on those three elements. The series, called *The Bones and the Blue*, included *Pelvis with the Moon* and *Pelvis II*.

During the war years, Stieglitz's health deteriorated. O'Keeffe continued to pursue her painting, but it was increasingly difficult for her to leave her aging husband each summer.

She wrote to a friend, Henry McBride:

> I see Alfred as an old man that I am very fond of—growing older—so that it sometimes shocks and startles me when he looks particularly pale and tired. . . . Aside from my fondness for him personally I feel that he has been something that has made my world for me—I like it that I can make him feel that I have hold of his hand to steady him as he goes on.[123]

O'Keeffe realized that she would soon be facing life without Stieglitz. She also knew that what she wanted more than anything else was to live out her days in New Mexico.

repainted white. The exhibit included paintings from every period of O'Keeffe's career, boasting sixty-one works dating from 1915 to 1941. In the exhibition's catalog, Rich wrote: "Seen in the whole her art betrays a perfect consistency. It has undergone no marked changes of style but has moved outward from its center. In over a quarter of a century of painting, O'Keeffe has only grown more herself."[122]

As the war raged in both Europe and the Pacific, O'Keeffe continued to divide her life between New Mexico and New York. Wartime rationing of gasoline made

9 "My Spirit Will Walk Here . . ."

In May 1945 O'Keeffe returned to New Mexico, where she purchased a second home, an abandoned hacienda-style building on three acres of land in Abiquiu, about sixteen miles from Ghost Ranch. The Abiquiu house was in ruins and required extensive renovations over the next three years, but the new location provided many benefits. The better soil enabled O'Keeffe to grow her own fruits and vegetables, and she no longer had to pump her own water.

O'Keeffe created an all-white studio with glass walls so that she could gaze down on the beautiful Chama River valley.

The patio of O'Keeffe's home in Abiquiu, New Mexico, which she purchased in a state of ruin. The home required extensive remodeling.

The interior of the house was finished in dark gray adobe. It was the tradition for women to apply the smooth finish, and this pleased her immensely. In a letter to a friend, she wrote:

> This morning the women started the smooth coat of plaster—It was a bright clear day and is quite wonderful— women on scaffolds against the sky . . . men mixing a vast pile of mud for the women to plaster with. It is really beautiful to see and the mud surface made with the hand makes one want to touch.[124]

O'Keeffe furnished the house simply with wooden benches. It was her creation, and everything in the dwelling reflected her simple tastes.

When the war ended in 1945, the mood of the country lifted. No longer preoccupied with a massive war effort, the United States focused on domestic issues. O'Keeffe was one of ten women—scientists, business leaders, and other notable achievers—chosen by the Women's National Press Club as 1945's "Makers and Promoters of Progress."

The nation was finally experiencing a period of economic recovery. To trumpet this renewed optimism, the Museum of Modern Art launched a major retrospective of O'Keeffe's work in May 1946. The July 6, 1946, issue of the *Saturday Review* carried a review by James Thrall Soby that said in part:

> Her imagery is singularly compelling. Indeed, I can remember few large exhibition openings like hers recently at which the pictures came out to get you and did not let you go, despite the distraction of people and manners.[125]

After the exhibit's successful opening, O'Keeffe's thoughts turned to New Mexico once again, but she was ambivalent about leaving Stieglitz that year. More than eighty years old, he had been suffering from angina and was weak and frail. He spent most of his days on a cot in the rear of An American Place, greeting the few visitors who stopped by. Although O'Keeffe encouraged friends to visit her husband, a new wave of European painters, including the Russian Marc Chagall and the German Max Ernst, had captured the imagination of the country's art disciples. Stieglitz was seen as an eccentric old man.

As always, the pull of New Mexico was strong. In June, O'Keeffe decided to return to Abiquiu. She had been there only a few weeks when she learned that Stieglitz had suffered a massive stroke. She caught the first available flight to New York, but by the time she reached Doctor's Hospital, Stieglitz had lapsed into a coma. He died on July 13, 1946.

Life Without Stieglitz

O'Keeffe selected a plain pine coffin for her husband. She sat up much of the night before the funeral, removing the pink satin lining and replacing it with white linen. The body was cremated, and O'Keeffe traveled alone to Lake George, where she privately buried the remains. "I put him where he could hear the Lake," she later wrote.[126]

When O'Keeffe wrote a text to accompany a collection of her husband's photographs of her, she recalled the man who had played such an important role in her life:

> For me he was much more wonderful in his work than as a human being. I believe it was the work that kept me with him—though I loved him as a human being. I could see his strengths and weaknesses. I put up with what seemed to me a good deal of contradictory nonsense because of what seemed clear and bright and wonderful.[127]

Stieglitz shortly before his death in 1946. Although she knew that he was gravely ill, O'Keeffe nonetheless took her usual trip to New Mexico.

The 1946 Retrospective

In 1946 the Museum of Modern Art held a major retrospective of O'Keeffe's works. James Thrall Soby, art critic for the Saturday Review, *wrote this review of the exhibit, excerpted here from* Georgia O'Keeffe *by Michael Berry.*

"Georgia O'Keeffe, perhaps the greatest of living women painters, is now having a retrospective exhibition at the Museum of Modern Art in New York. I must admit that looking at her pictures year after year at Stieglitz's gallery, I did not know consistently whether I liked them or not. A few weeks ago, after seeing so much of her life work at the Museum, my doubts vanished. I think Miss O'Keeffe creates a world. It is a world of surprising variety. Sometimes her painting seems an art of psychic confession, an inner recital of symbolic language, like the murmur of acolytes. Then again it becomes more objective and she paints the mountains of New Mexico as though they answered when she spoke. Throughout her work there is a dual conception of nature: nature as the painter herself; and nature as an unfailing companion with whom she converses in terms of wonderful precision, intimacy, and shades of meaning. In subject matter she turns her back on humanity, but there is love in her work, courage, strength, devotion.

Her imagery is singularly compelling. Indeed, I can remember few large exhibition openings like hers recently at which the pictures came out to get you and did not let you go, despite the distraction of people and manners. Hers is a world of exceptional intensity: bones and flowers, hills and the city, sometimes abstract and vigorous, sometimes warm and fugitive. She created this world; it was not there before; and there is nothing like it anywhere."

Publicly, O'Keeffe conducted herself with an air of calm acceptance over Stieglitz's death, but privately she felt a profound guilt over leaving her husband that summer. There was little time to grieve, however: As the primary heir and sole executrix of her husband's will, she was faced with the immense task of dispersing Stieglitz's estate, including his large art collection. There were 850 works of modern art, hundreds of photographs, and fifty thousand letters. For the next three years O'Keeffe devoted herself to the task of settling the estate. The bulk of

Stieglitz's belongings went to the Metropolitan Museum of Art in New York City, with the second-largest lot going to the Art Institute of Chicago.

O'Keeffe painted little during the years she executed Stieglitz's will. Before she left New York, where she had spent at least half of the last thirty years, she painted the Brooklyn Bridge, a structure completed just four years before her birth. After this farewell gesture to the city that had accepted her as a respected artist, she moved permanently to New Mexico, residing in her Abiquiu home during the winter and spring and at Rancho de los Burros during summer and autumn.

Living Her Dream

At last O'Keeffe was free to live the life she had dreamed about for so many years. For the first time she experienced winters in New Mexico. Invigorated by the snowy landscapes, she painted with renewed passion. Her best-known work of 1948 was *In the Patio II*, a simple composition featuring a window of her adobe dwelling juxtaposed against a brilliant blue sky.

As always, O'Keeffe enjoyed being alone, but when a friend gave her two chow pups, Bo and Chia, she grew to love the dogs. Known for their fiercely protective dispositions, the animals guarded O'Keeffe against intruders, becoming her loyal companions.

The sixty-two-year-old O'Keeffe became the recipient of more honors and awards. In 1949 she was elected to the National Institute of Arts and Letters. Few women had won this honor and she was especially proud to be elected by the membership, which was 90 percent male. She felt the

O'Keeffe at the ceremony in which she was inducted into the National Institute of Arts and Letters. At the time, very few women artists were members of the institute.

award proved that the male-dominated art world had accepted her and respected her work. More important, she believed that her election paved the way for a wider acceptance of female artists.

Seeing the World

O'Keeffe had never left the United States except for brief trips to Canada and Hawaii, which was not a state in 1938, when she had visited in connection with the commission from Dole. As the second half of the twentieth century arrived, however, she began to explore new parts of the world. Crossing the border into Mexico in 1951, she was fascinated by the carnival colors in the peasant markets.

In 1953 O'Keeffe traveled to Paris and toured the rest of France before continuing on to Spain. There she saw the Prado, the National Museum of Painting and

Sculpture housing more than two thousand paintings by Spanish and foreign masters. O'Keeffe particularly admired the works of Francisco Goya. In 1956 she visited Peru and described the country: "The colors there are almost unbelievable . . . marvelous, purples, violent colors. And the Andes are sparkling—they freeze at night, and in the morning they glitter. I think it's the most beautiful country I've ever seen."[128]

O'Keeffe traveled around the world in 1959. As a young woman, she had gone by train, viewing the scenery at eye level. Flying gave her a new perspective on art as well as life:

It is breathtaking as one rises up over the world one has been living in . . . and looks down at it stretching away and away. The Rio Grande—the mountains—then the pattern of rivers. . . . Then little lakes . . . then . . . Amarillo country . . . a fascinating restrained pattern of different greens and cooler browns. . . . It is very handsome way off into the level distance,

Reflections on Painting

Georgia O'Keeffe was born to be a painter. She thrived on her work and found it to be the most important part of her life. In 1962, in an interview with writer Lee Nordness published in Art: USA, *she described the importance of painting.*

"One works I suppose because it is the most interesting thing that one knows to do.

The days one works are the best days. On the other days one is hurrying through the other things one has to do to keep one's life going.

You get the garden planted. You get the roof fixed. You take the dog to the vet. You spend the day with a friend. You learn to make a new kind of bread. You hunt up photographs for someone who thinks he needs them. You certainly have to do the shopping.

You may even enjoy doing such things. You think they have to be done. You even think you have to have some visitors or take a trip to keep from getting queer living alone with just two chows. But always you are hurrying through these so that you can get at the painting again because that is the high spot—in a way it is what you do all the other things for. Why it is that way I do not know.

I have no theories to offer. The painting is like a thread that runs through all the reasons for all the other things that make one's life."

fantastically handsome. . . . The world all simplified and beautiful and clear-cut in patterns like time and history will simplify and straighten out these times of ours—What one sees from the air is so simple and so beautiful I cannot help feeling that it would do something wonderful for the human race—rid it of much smallness and pettishness if more people flew.[129]

New Inspirations for Painting

Flying focused O'Keeffe's artistic inspiration on the sky. In two huge canvases, *From the Plains, I* and *II* (1955), she recalled her years in Texas, depicting an orange sky charged with jagged lightning bolts. In *Ladder to the Moon* (1958), New Mexico's Pedernal provides a backdrop for a ladder stretching to a half-visible moon, all elements suggesting transition just as the artist, at seventy-one, sensed a shift to the final stage of her life.

In 1960 O'Keeffe's friend Daniel Catton Rich, now director of the Worcester (Massachusetts) Art Museum, arranged for an exhibition of her works. Many of the works exhibited in Worcester reflected her intrigue with perspectives from the sky. Some viewers misunderstood the compositions' theme, but O'Keeffe was pleased when she overheard the remark of one patron. "One day I saw a man looking around at my showing," she wrote in her autobiography. "'They must be rivers seen from the air.' I was pleased that someone had seen what I saw and remembered it my way."[130]

During a flight in 1960 O'Keeffe described the view from the plane's window: "Now the sun is bright over what looks like a vast field of snow stretching all the way to the horizon. It is odd to look out on this field of snow or white cotton—It looks almost solid enough to walk on."[131] O'Keeffe later told a friend that she could not wait to get home to paint what she had seen. This scene served as the inspiration for a series of huge paintings, *Sky Above Clouds*, completed between 1963 and 1965.

The largest painting of the series and of O'Keeffe's career, *Sky Above Clouds IV*, measures twenty-four feet by eight feet and was completed in 1965, when the artist was nearly seventy-eight. O'Keeffe began working on the composition in June. Painting the massive canvas during the summer in an unheated garage, O'Keeffe pushed herself to complete the composition before the cold set in. By working long hours every day, she was able to complete the work before autumn. Later she recalled the project:

I had two 10-foot tables with a board between [in order] to be high enough

O'Keeffe, in her seventies, walks in her Abiquiu garden. Even at this age, O'Keeffe worked long hours at her art.

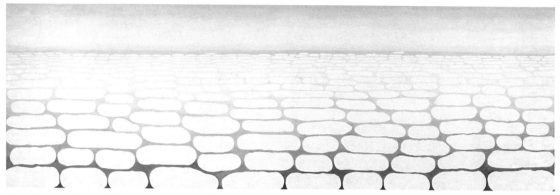

Sky Above Clouds IV, part of her clouds series. The painting is immense, twenty-four feet by eight feet. It depicts the sky as O'Keeffe had seen it from the air during an airplane flight in 1960.

to reach the top of the canvas. First, I stood on the tables. Then I sat on a chair on the tables. After that I sat on the tables. Then I moved the tables and stood on a plank and after that I sat on the floor to reach the bottom.[132]

This massive composition and the work required to complete it demonstrated what O'Keeffe had told an interviewer: "I don't think I have a great gift, it isn't just talent. You have to have something else. You have to have a kind of nerve. It's mostly a lot of very, very hard work."[133]

Sky Above Clouds IV was included in a 1966 exhibit of O'Keeffe's works at the Amon Carter Museum of Western Art in Forth Worth, Texas. Parts of the exhibit later traveled to the University of New Mexico in Albuquerque, where the residents of her adopted state could finally see the first major exhibit of her works in New Mexico.

America Honors O'Keeffe

As America sought to honor the artist who was so admired and respected, O'Keeffe was elected to the fifty-member American Academy of Arts and Letters, the nation's highest honor society for men and women in the arts. In 1968 *Life* magazine featured O'Keeffe in a generously illustrated cover story, and in 1970 New York's Whitney Museum opened an O'Keeffe retrospective.

Not only did Americans admire O'-Keeffe as artist, but her strong sense of independence fit the ideal of the American character. She had never cared what others thought of her, and as an elderly woman, she retained and strengthened that attitude. Her admirers respected her firm opinions. "Georgia is easy to get along with," quipped a museum director, "as long as she gets exactly what she wants."[134]

As O'Keeffe neared the eighth decade of her life, her singular appearance was more striking than ever. The New Mexico sun had etched in her face deep lines that were accentuated by her black clothing. She stood proud and erect, her white hair pulled back in a tight knot, and spoke with the confidence and wisdom of an octogenarian. Admirers began to flock to her Abiquiu ranch, where they would simply show up at the door to meet the famous

In 1970 an aging O'Keeffe stands before a painting she completed in 1928. Upon learning that her eyesight was worsening, O'Keeffe stopped painting for several years.

Juan Hamilton's Friendship

In 1972 Juan Hamilton, a young potter, appeared at O'Keeffe's door, looking for odd jobs. Although the artist did not like to have many people around, she realized that the young man could help her with the wrapping and shipping of paintings. She grew to like Hamilton and increasingly relied on his assistance. Gradually, Hamilton and O'Keeffe became good friends as well. They encouraged each other's artistic endeavors, and Hamilton persuaded O'Keeffe to try her hand at pottery. He felt the medium suited the aging artist because of her failing eyesight. "As I watched him work with the clay I saw that he could make it speak," O'Keeffe wrote in her autobiography. "I hadn't thought much about pottery but now I thought that maybe I could make a pot, too—maybe a beautiful pot—it could become another language for me."[136] While O'Keeffe briefly tried her hand at pottery, she picked up her brushes again, painting *From a Day with Juan and Green Spring*.

Although O'Keeffe had written simple but powerful exhibition catalog entries and beautiful letters to her friends over the years, she had never enjoyed writing. With Hamilton's encouragement, she completed her autobiography, which was published in 1976. *Georgia O'Keeffe* featured more than a hundred color reproductions of her work and received excellent reviews. Reviewer Sanford Schwartz wrote that the work, like its subject, was both "casual and regal."[137]

To honor O'Keeffe on her ninetieth birthday in 1977, the Public Broadcasting System aired a television documentary

artist. According to her mood, O'Keeffe might greet strangers warmly, serving them a cup of tea in her kitchen. At other times she opened the gate, snapped "Front side," and, turning on her heel, barked "Back side!" slamming the gate as she shouted, "Goodbye!"[135]

The only profound physical affliction that plagued O'Keeffe in her later years was the loss of her sharp eyesight. Doctors informed her that she had lost her central vision as a result of deterioration due to aging. She would be able to see only peripherally, from the corners of her eyes. This news threw O'Keeffe into a deep depression. She did not paint for several years.

Remembering Stieglitz

In 1978 the Metropolitan Museum of Art published Georgia O'Keeffe: A Portrait by Alfred Stieglitz, an intriguing collection of Stieglitz's photographs of O'Keeffe, who wrote a beautiful text to accompany the graphic material. Here, she remembers her husband and their relationship.

"Thirty years have passed since I sorted out the Alfred Stieglitz photographs and made the key set which consists of the best prints that he kept mounted of every negative that he had printed. . . .

I was able to know more than anyone else—both the worst and the best about him. He was either loved or hated—there wasn't much in between.

He gave a flight to the spirit and faith in their own way to more people—particularly young people—than anyone I have known.

He thought aloud and his opinion about anything in the middle morning might be quite different by afternoon, so that people quoting him might make quite contradictory statements. There was such a power when he spoke—people seemed to believe what he said, even when they knew it wasn't their truth. He molded his hearer. They were often left speechless. If they crossed him in any way, his power to destroy was as destructive as his power to build—the extremes went together. I have experienced both and survived, but I think I only crossed him when I had to survive.

There was a constant grinding like the ocean. It was as if someone hot, dark, and destructive was hitched to the highest, brightest star."

O'Keeffe and Stieglitz pose before some of O'Keeffe's works.

(Left) O'Keeffe with Mrs. Walter Mondale shortly before O'Keeffe's ninetieth birthday. They are at the National Gallery of Art in Washington, D.C. (Below, left) O'Keeffe took up pottery in her eighties as a new artistic endeavor that did not require keen eyesight.

and O'Keeffe wrote the introduction for *Georgia O'Keeffe: A Portrait by Alfred Stieglitz,* published the same year.

Although she was frail, O'Keeffe declared that she would live to be a hundred. She had lived a full life, and reflecting on her accomplishments gave her great satisfaction. With the help of Hamilton and her staff, she still enjoyed her dogs, the successors of Bo and Chia, and the simple pleasures of life: her garden, a well-cooked meal, and the beauty of the desert. When she reached age ninety-eight in November 1985, it seemed that she might achieve her goal of living for a century. But three months later she weakened. On March 6, 1986, she was taken to a hospital in Santa Fe, where she died.

In discussing her feelings about death and the beliefs of New Mexico's Indians, O'Keeffe had once said, "When I think of death, I only regret that I will not be able to see this beautiful country anymore, unless the Indians are right and my spirit will walk here after I'm gone."[138]

about her life and career. In 1978 the Metropolitan Museum of Art exhibited a collection of fifty-one of Stieglitz's photographs. The museum published a collection of photographs from the exhibit,

Courage and Vision

To embark on a study of Georgia O'Keeffe is to open a door revealing color, imagination, courage, and vision. These elements are O'Keeffe, and they speak to today's viewer as clearly as they did at the beginning of the twentieth century when this remarkable woman and artist began her work.

The most obscure forms of nature inspired O'Keeffe, and in transferring her inspirations to canvas, she inspired others to share her perception of the magnificent beauty in the smallest flower, in an animal skull, a barn, or a river, in the desert, or in the sky. The viewer is transported to some unexplored vantage point, which enables one to see what O'Keeffe envisioned in her unique way.

The enduring spirit of Georgia O'Keeffe lives in the story of her life as it does through her works. Born in an era when women were little more than property, she had the good fortune to be encouraged to aspire to a different life. Through the example of the strong women in her family, she established a vision for herself; through the greatest adversity, she remained true to that mission. O'Keeffe also possessed the courage to listen to her intuitive voice and not to surrender her sense of self to traditional or popular conventions.

The deep lines and craggy features etched into her face after years in the New Mexico sun can clearly be seen in this portrait of O'Keeffe taken shortly before her death.

Georgia O'Keeffe became an American poet on canvas, capturing the very essence of the country in its natural wonders and embodying the courage of a pioneer in exploring undiscovered forms. Her efforts required a brave spirit and a unique vision. As James Soby had said: "Hers is a world of exceptional intensity: . . . sometimes abstract and vigorous, sometimes warm and fugitive. She created this world; it was not there before; and there is nothing like it anywhere."[139]

Notes

Introduction: An Enduring Vision

1. Quoted in Katherine Hoffman, *An Enduring Spirit: The Art of Georgia O'Keeffe.* Metuchen, NJ: Scarecrow Press, 1984.
2. Robert Hughes, "Loner in the Desert," *Time*, October 12, 1970.

Chapter 1: Color, Light, and Pattern

3. Quoted in Roxana Robinson, *Georgia O'Keeffe: A Life.* New York: Harper & Row, 1989.
4. Quoted in Robinson, *Georgia O'Keeffe: A Life.*
5. Quoted in Robinson, *Georgia O'Keeffe: A Life.*
6. Quoted in Robinson, *Georgia O'Keeffe: A Life.*
7. Quoted in Robinson, *Georgia O'Keeffe: A Life.*
8. Quoted in Robinson, *Georgia O'Keeffe: A Life.*
9. Quoted in Robinson, *Georgia O'Keeffe: A Life.*
10. Laurie Lisle, *Portrait of an Artist: A Biography of Georgia O'Keeffe.* New York: Seaview Books, 1980.
11. Quoted in Beverly Gherman, *Georgia O'Keeffe: The "Wideness and Wonder" of Her World.* New York: Atheneum, 1986.
12. Quoted in Robinson, *Georgia O'Keeffe: A Life.*
13. Robinson, *Georgia O'Keeffe: A Life.*
14. Quoted in Robinson, *Georgia O'Keeffe: A Life.*
15. Quoted in Robinson, *Georgia O'Keeffe: A Life.*
16. Quoted in Robinson, *Georgia O'Keeffe: A Life.*
17. Quoted in Robinson, *Georgia O'Keeffe: A Life.*
18. Quoted in Robinson, *Georgia O'Keeffe: A Life.*
19. Quoted in Gherman, *Georgia O'Keeffe.*

Chapter 2: A Budding Artist

20. Quoted in Robinson, *Georgia O'Keeffe: A Life.*
21. Quoted in Lisle, *Portrait of an Artist.*
22. Quoted in Lisle, *Portrait of an Artist.*
23. Quoted in Benita Eisler, *O'Keeffe and Stieglitz: An American Romance.* Garden City, NY: Doubleday, 1991.
24. Quoted in Robinson, *Georgia O'Keeffe: A Life.*
25. Quoted in Lisle, *Portrait of an Artist.*

26. Quoted in Robinson, *Georgia O'Keeffe: A Life.*
27. Quoted in Robinson, *Georgia O'Keeffe: A Life.*
28. Quoted in Robinson, *Georgia O'Keeffe: A Life.*
29. Robinson, *Georgia O'Keeffe: A Life.*
30. Quoted in Robinson, *Georgia O'Keeffe: A Life.*

Chapter 3: The Nonconformist

31. Quoted in Robinson, *Georgia O'Keeffe: A Life.*
32. Quoted in Ronald G. Pisano, *William Merritt Chase.* New York: Watson-Guptill, 1986.
33. Quoted in Robinson, *Georgia O'Keeffe: A Life.*
34. Quoted in Pisano, *William Merritt Chase.*
35. In Metropolitan Museum of Art, *Georgia O'Keeffe: A Portrait by Alfred Stieglitz.* Introduction by Georgia O'Keeffe. New York: Viking, 1978.
36. In Metropolitan Museum of Art, *Georgia O'Keeffe: A Portrait by Alfred Stieglitz.*
37. In Metropolitan Museum of Art, *Georgia O'Keeffe: A Portrait by Alfred Stieglitz.*
38. In Metropolitan Museum of Art, *Georgia O'Keeffe: A Portrait by Alfred Stieglitz.*
39. Georgia O'Keeffe, *Georgia O'Keeffe.* New York: Viking, 1976.
40. Quoted in Robinson, *Georgia O'Keeffe: A Life.*
41. Quoted in Robinson, *Georgia O'Keeffe: A Life.*
42. Quoted in Robinson, *Georgia O'Keeffe: A Life.*
43. Quoted in Robinson, *Georgia O'Keeffe: A Life.*
44. Quoted in Robinson, *Georgia O'Keeffe: A Life.*

Chapter 4: "A Thing of Your Own"

45. Quoted in Lisle, *Portrait of an Artist.*
46. Quoted in Lisle, *Portrait of an Artist.*
47. Quoted in Lisle, *Portrait of an Artist.*
48. Quoted in Robinson, *Georgia O'Keeffe: A Life.*
49. Quoted in Robinson, *Georgia O'Keeffe: A Life.*
50. Quoted in Robinson, *Georgia O'Keeffe: A Life.*
51. Michael Berry, *Georgia O'Keeffe.* New York: Chelsea House, 1988.
52. Quoted in Robinson, *Georgia O'Keeffe: A Life.*
53. Anita Pollitzer, *A Woman on Paper: Georgia*

O'Keeffe. New York: Simon & Schuster, 1988.

54. Quoted in Robinson, *Georgia O'Keeffe: A Life*.

55. Quoted in Pollitzer, *A Woman on Paper*.

56. Quoted in Robinson, *Georgia O'Keeffe: A Life*.

57. Quoted in Robinson, *Georgia O'Keeffe: A Life*.

58. Quoted in Pollitzer, *A Woman on Paper*.

59. Quoted in Pollitzer, *A Woman on Paper*.

60. Quoted in Lisle, *Portrait of an Artist*.

Chapter 5: "A Woman on Paper"

61. Quoted in Lisle, *Portrait of an Artist*.

62. Quoted in Mitchell A. Wilder, ed., *Georgia O'Keeffe: An Exhibition of the Work of the Artist from 1915 to 1966*. Fort Worth, TX: Amon Carter Museum of Western Art, 1966.

63. Quoted in Gherman, *Georgia O'Keeffe*.

64. Quoted in Pollitzer, *A Woman on Paper*.

65. Quoted in Robinson, *Georgia O'Keeffe: A Life*.

66. Quoted in Robinson, *Georgia O'Keeffe: A Life*.

67. Quoted in Robinson, *Georgia O'Keeffe: A Life*.

68. Quoted in Robinson, *Georgia O'Keeffe: A Life*.

69. Quoted in Wilder, *Georgia O'Keeffe: An Exhibition of the Work of the Artist from 1915 to 1966*.

70. Henry Tyrell, quoted in Robinson, *Georgia O'Keeffe: A Life*.

71. Quoted in Robinson, *Georgia O'Keeffe: A Life*.

72. In Metropolitan Museum of Art, *Georgia O'Keeffe: A Portrait by Alfred Stieglitz*.

73. Quoted in Lisle, *Portrait of an Artist*.

74. Quoted in Lisle, *Portrait of an Artist*.

75. In Metropolitan Museum of Art, *Georgia O'Keeffe: A Portrait by Alfred Stieglitz*.

76. Quoted in Pollitzer, *A Woman on Paper*.

Chapter 6: Invading a Man's World

77. Quoted in Robinson, *Georgia O'Keeffe: A Life*.

78. In Metropolitan Museum of Art, *Georgia O'Keeffe: A Portrait by Alfred Stieglitz*.

79. Quoted in Robinson, *Georgia O'Keeffe: A Life*.

80. In Metropolitan Museum of Art, *Georgia O'Keeffe: A Portrait by Alfred Stieglitz*.

81. In Metropolitan Museum of Art, *Georgia O'Keeffe: A Portrait by Alfred Stieglitz*.

82. Quoted in Robinson, *Georgia O'Keeffe: A Life*.

83. Quoted in Robinson, *Georgia O'Keeffe: A Life*.

84. Quoted in Robinson, *Georgia O'Keeffe: A Life*.

85. Quoted in Robinson, *Georgia O'Keeffe: A Life*.

86. Quoted in Robinson, *Georgia O'Keeffe: A Life*.

87. Quoted in Gherman, *Georgia O'Keeffe*.

88. Quoted in Robinson, *Georgia O'Keeffe: A Life*.

89. Quoted in Robinson, *Georgia O'Keeffe: A Life*.

90. Quoted in Robinson, *Georgia O'Keeffe: A Life*.

91. Quoted in Robinson, *Georgia O'Keeffe: A Life*.

92. Quoted in Wilder, *Georgia O'Keeffe: An Exhibition of the Work of the Artist from 1915 to 1966*.

93. Quoted in Robinson, *Georgia O'Keeffe: A Life*.

94. Quoted in Lisle, *Portrait of an Artist*.

95. Quoted in Robinson, *Georgia O'Keeffe: A Life*.

96. Quoted in Robinson, *Georgia O'Keeffe: A Life*.

97. Quoted in Robinson, *Georgia O'Keeffe: A Life*.

Chapter 7: Transitions

98. Quoted in Robinson, *Georgia O'Keeffe: A Life*.

99. Quoted in Robinson, *Georgia O'Keeffe: A Life*.

100. Quoted in Robinson, *Georgia O'Keeffe: A Life*.

101. Quoted in Gherman, *Georgia O'Keeffe*.

102. Quoted in Robinson, *Georgia O'Keeffe: A Life*.

103. Quoted in Berry, *Georgia O'Keeffe*.

104. Quoted in Berry, *Georgia O'Keeffe*.

105. Quoted in Lisa Mintz Messinger, *Georgia O'Keeffe*. New York: Thames and Hudson and the Metropolitan Museum of Art, 1988.

106. Quoted in Wilder, *Georgia O'Keeffe: An Exhibition of the Work of the Artist from 1915 to 1966*.

107. Quoted in Hoffman, *An Enduring Spirit*.

108. Quoted in Robinson, *Georgia O'Keeffe: A Life*.

109. Quoted in Robinson, *Georgia O'Keeffe: A Life*.

Chapter 8: New Mexico

110. Quoted in Robinson, *Georgia O'Keeffe: A Life*.

111. Quoted in Robinson, *Georgia O'Keeffe: A Life*.

112. Quoted in Hoffman, *An Enduring Spirit*.

113. Quoted in Robinson, *Georgia O'Keeffe: A Life*.

114. Quoted in Robinson, *Georgia O'Keeffe: A Life*.

115. Quoted in Robinson, *Georgia O'Keeffe: A Life*.

116. Quoted in Berry, *Georgia O'Keeffe*.

117. Quoted in Berry, *Georgia O'Keeffe*.

118. Quoted in Berry, *Georgia O'Keeffe*.

119. Quoted in Berry, *Georgia O'Keeffe.*

120. Quoted in Messinger, *Georgia O'Keeffe.*

121. Quoted in Berry, *Georgia O'Keeffe.*

122. Quoted in Lisle, *Portrait of an Artist.*

123. Quoted in Hoffman, *An Enduring Spirit.*

Chapter 9: "My Spirit Will Walk Here . . ."

124. Quoted in Robinson, *Georgia O'Keeffe: A Life.*

125. Quoted in Wilder, *Georgia O'Keeffe: An Exhibition of the Work of the Artist from 1915 to 1966.*

126. Quoted in Robinson, *Georgia O'Keeffe: A Life.*

127. In Metropolitan Museum of Art, *Georgia O'Keeffe: A Portrait by Alfred Stieglitz.*

128. Quoted in Robinson, *Georgia O'Keeffe: A Life.*

129. Quoted in Robinson, *Georgia O'Keeffe: A Life.*

130. Quoted in Berry, *Georgia O'Keeffe.*

131. Quoted in Robinson, *Georgia O'Keeffe: A Life.*

132. Quoted in Robinson, *Georgia O'Keeffe: A Life.*

133. Quoted in Gherman, *Georgia O'Keeffe.*

134. Quoted in Gherman, *Georgia O'Keeffe.*

135. Quoted in Berry, *Georgia O'Keeffe.*

136. Quoted in Berry, *Georgia O'Keeffe.*

137. Quoted in Berry, *Georgia O'Keeffe.*

138. Quoted in Berry, *Georgia O'Keeffe.*

Epilogue: Courage and Vision

139. Quoted in Berry, *Georgia O'Keeffe.*

For Further Reading

Michael Berry, *Georgia O'Keeffe*. New York: Chelsea House, 1988. A young adult biography providing a very readable account of O'Keeffe's life. Includes chronology, further readings, index, many photographs, and some color prints.

Nicholas Calloway, ed., *One Hundred Flowers*. New York: Knopf, 1987. A beautiful color collection of one hundred of O'Keeffe's flower paintings with an afterword by the editor.

Beverly Gherman, *Georgia O'Keeffe: The "Wideness and Wonder" of Her World*. New York: Atheneum, 1986. A juvenile biography containing some black-and-white photographs. The sparse text is rich with well-cited O'Keeffe quotations. Includes a bibliography and index.

Katherine Hoffman, *An Enduring Spirit: The Art of Georgia O'Keeffe*. Metuchen, NJ: Scarecrow Press, 1984. This fascinating study of the artist and her works divides O'Keeffe's artistic accomplishments into historical periods, artistic movements, topics such as the feminist movement, and O'Keeffe's treatment of nature. Contains some black-and-white prints. The excellent text is filled with quotations that are cited. The book contains a preface, prologue, epilogue, bibliography, and index.

Laurie Lisle, *Portrait of an Artist: A Biography of Georgia O'Keeffe*. New York: Seaview Books, 1980. Drawing on three years of interviews with friends, relatives, and colleagues, and O'Keeffe's vast collection of correspondence, Lisle presents a full portrait of O'Keeffe. No photographs.

Metropolitan Museum of Art, *Georgia O'Keeffe: A Portrait by Alfred Stieglitz*. New York: Viking, 1978. An intriguing collection of Stieglitz's photographs of O'Keeffe with a brief yet fascinating text by O'Keeffe.

Georgia O'Keeffe, *Georgia O'Keeffe*. New York: Viking, 1976. A color collection of O'Keeffe's works with a brief but beautifully written text.

Anita Pollitzer, *A Woman on Paper: Georgia O'Keeffe*. New York: Simon & Schuster, 1988. Using as a foundation the correspondence between O'Keeffe and the author, a lifelong friend, the book offers a unique perspective on O'Keeffe's life and her passion for her work.

Roxana Robinson. *Georgia O'Keeffe: A Life*. New York: Harper & Row, 1989. An all-encompassing biography of O'Keeffe, filled with quotations and excerpts from correspondence. Robinson has provided a complete examination of O'Keeffe's life. Contains no photographs, but includes complete bibliographic listing and index.

Film

Georgia O'Keeffe, documentary film produced and directed by Perry Miller Adato for WNET/13, the Public Broadcasting Service, 1977.

Additional Works Consulted

Willa Cather, *My Antonia.* 1918. Reprint. Garden City, NY: International Collectors Library, 1954.

Emmett Dedmon, *A Great City's History and People.* New York: Atheneum, 1981. A historical overview of Chicago covering the period 1835–1981. Divided into five historical periods.

Benita Eisler, *O'Keeffe and Stieglitz: An American Romance.* Garden City, NY: Doubleday, 1991. An in-depth examination of the relationship between Alfred Stieglitz and O'Keeffe as well as their complex connections with their friends Rebecca and Paul Strand. Contains photographs not published in earlier works, full citations, a bibliography, and an index.

Charles C. Eldredge, *Georgia O'Keeffe.* New York: Harry N. Abrams, 1991. A beautiful collection of O'Keeffe's works produced on quality paper and accompanied by an ample text. It features a chronology and an index.

Ann Sutherland Harris and Linda Nochlin, *Women Artists: 1550–1950.* New York: Los Angeles County Museum of Art and Alfred A. Knopf, 1976. A collection of brief biographies and selected works by women artists over four hundred years. Several pages are devoted to O'Keeffe, accompanied by black-and-white photographs and descriptions of the selected works.

Jeffrey Hogrefe, *O'Keeffe: The Life of an American Legend.* New York: Bantam Books, 1992. From O'Keeffe's early poverty to her mental collapse to her tragic loss of eyesight in her later years that robbed this great artist of her visual world, Hogrefe offers an in-depth look at O'Keeffe as woman and artist.

Robert Hughes, "Loner in the Desert," *Time,* October 12, 1970.

Lisa Mintz Messinger, *Georgia O'Keeffe.* New York: Thames and Hudson and the Metropolitan Museum of Art, 1988. A fascinating collection of O'Keeffe's works in both color and black and white, accompanied by an informative text. Contains an introduction, notes, chronology, and index.

Sarah Whitaker Peters, *Becoming O'Keeffe: The Early Works.* New York: Abbeville Press, 1991. A biography limited to O'Keeffe's early years, also features black-and-white and color photographs, notes, a bibliography, and an index.

Ronald G. Pisano, *William Merritt Chase.* New York: Watson-Guptill, 1986. A color collection of Chase's art, complete with ample text.

Mitchell A. Wilder, ed., *Georgia O'Keeffe: An Exhibition of the Work of the Artist from 1915 to 1966.* Fort Worth, TX: Amon Carter Museum of Western Art, 1966. A unique collection of entries from O'Keeffe's exhibition catalogs from 1915 to 1966 as well as some reviews by various critics. The works are fully cited and are accompanied by several black-and-white prints.

Nancy Woloch, *Women and the American Experience.* New York: Knopf, 1984. A compilation of both historic periods and the influential women who shaped American history—from the frontier to current times. Includes preface, index, appendix, and biographical notes.

Index

Picture Credits

About the Author

Lois P. Nicholson is a native of Sudlersville, Maryland. She holds a bachelor of science degree in elementary education and a master's degree in education from the Salisbury State University. She is a media specialist in an elementary school near Annapolis, Maryland. She has written *Cal Ripken, Jr.: Quiet Hero, George Washington Carver, Oprah Winfrey, Helen Keller, Michael Jackson, Casey Stengel, Nolan Ryan, Lucille Ball,* and *Babe Ruth.* In addition to writing, Nicholson visits schools and speaks to students and faculties about the writing of nonfiction. Lois Nicholson is the mother of two grown children and lives in Baltimore, Maryland.

--
B
Okeeffe
N

Nicholson, Lois, 19 93
1949-

Georgia O'Keeffe.

DATE			